# POPE FRANCIS
# Deacons
## SERVANTS OF CHARITY

Deacon Enzo Petrolino

Foreword by Pope Francis

United States Conference of Catholic Bishops
Washington, DC

English translation of *Il Diaconato nel Pensiero di Papa Francesco: Una Chiesa povera per I poveri* (Vatican City: Libreria Editrice Vaticana, 2017).

First printing, July 2018

ISBN 978-1-60137-583-4

# Contents

# Foreword

In recent decades, the Church has experienced extraordinary spiritual and pastoral growth thanks to the deep reception of the documents from the Second Vatican Council. Numerous documents have been written by my predecessors, from Bl. Paul VI and St. John Paul II to Pope Benedict XVI, who expounded on the conciliar event. In this context, the *permanent diaconate* has rediscovered the roots of its presence in the community of believers and in the broader social fabric by acquiring awareness of its role of service to Christ and to humanity, and by receiving new impetus from the guidelines that the Magisterium has offered to common ecclesial reflection over the years.

I would like to offer my heartfelt thanks to the author, Enzo Petrolino, president of the Diaconate Community in Italy, who wished to gather my writings on the diaconate from my episcopal ministry in Buenos Aires and now, as Bishop of Rome.

Today, it is both interesting and necessary to examine in greater detail how the permanent diaconate has developed from its restoration to the present day, to better understand its *path*, through a reading that captures all of the doctrinal, pastoral, and exhortative richness of the discourse and various pronouncements that the Papal Magisterium has addressed to deacons all around the world in these post-conciliar years.

The Church sees in the permanent diaconate the expression and, at the same time, the vital impetus to become a visible sign of the diaconia of Christ the Servant in the history of mankind. The sensitivity to the formation of a *diaconal conscience* can truly be considered the underlying motive that must permeate Christian communities.

The service of the diaconal ministry finds its identity in evangelization, as St. John Paul II said in a homily in 1979 to a group of new deacons, reminding them of the presentation of the Book of the Gospels during Ordination: "'Receive the Gospel of Christ, whose herald you now are. Believe what you read, teach what you believe, and practice what you teach.' And so you are called to take the words of the Acts of the Apostles to heart. In the rank of deacons you have come to be associated with Peter and John and all the apostles. You support the apostolic ministry and share in its proclamation. Like the Apostles you too must feel impelled to proclaim by word and deed the Resurrection of the Lord Jesus. You too must experience the need to do good, to render service in the name of the crucified and Risen Jesus—to bring God's word into the lives of his holy people."[1]

Therefore, as I wrote in the Apostolic Exhortation *Evangelii Gaudium* (EG), it is a good thing that "priests,

---

1    Pope John Paul II, Homily for a Eucharistic Celebration with a Group of Deacons (April 21, 1979).

deacons, and the laity gather periodically to discover resources which can make preaching more attractive!"[2]

Another important aspect is praying for vocations. The faithful must assume their responsibility for the care and discernment of vocations, even for the diaconal ministry. When the Apostles sought someone to take the place of Judas Iscariot, St. Peter brought together a hundred and twenty of the brethren (cf. Acts 1:15); and in order to choose seven deacons, a group of disciples was gathered (cf. Acts 6:2). Still today, the Christian community is always present in the budding of vocations, in their formation and in their perseverance.[3]

Furthermore, all *diaconia* in the Church—of which ministerial diaconia is the sign and instrument—has its beating heart in the Eucharistic Mystery and is primarily realized through the service of the poor, who bear the face of Christ who suffers. When the emperor asked Deacon Lawrence—the administrator of the Diocese of Rome—to bring the riches of the diocese as payment to not be killed, he returned with the poor. The poor are the treasure of the Church. If you are the head of a bank but your heart is poor and not attached to the money, then it will always be at the service of others. "Poverty" is this detachment, to serve those in need, to serve others.

---

2    Pope Francis, Apostolic Exhortation *Evangelii Gaudium* (EG) (November 24, 2013), no. 159.

3    Cf. EG, no. 107.

Thus, a *Church which is poor and for the poor.* I have already mentioned that during the election, I was seated next to Cardinal Claudio Hummes, the Archbishop Emeritus of São Paolo and Prefect Emeritus of the Congregation for the Clergy! When I was elected pope, he gave me a hug and a kiss and said, "Don't forget the poor!" Then, right away, thinking of the poor, I thought of St. Francis of Assisi. That is how the name came into my heart: Francis, who tradition tells us was a deacon. For me, he is the man of poverty, the man of peace, the man who loves and protects creation. He is the man all deacons should be inspired by.

Throughout the different stages of the diaconal journey, the Papal Magisterium has left a clarifying and stimulating mark characterized by the faithful obedience and joy that must accompany the deacon's mission in the Church and in the world today, while broadening the directives indicated by the Council and extending their scope and the horizons of their action.

Those who work to promote the diaconal ministry, as well as those who exercise it, will find a lot of interesting information for a greater understanding and more in-depth study—even in a pastoral sense—of the identity and role of permanent deacons today in the author's many works published by the Libreria Editrice Vaticana, especially in *Nuovo Enchiridion sul Diaconato: Le fonti e i documenti ufficiali della Chiesa* (*The New Enchiridion on the Diaconate*), which I received from Deacon Petrolino during the audience for the International Diaconate Center on the occasion of their jubilee.

The diaconal ministry must be seen as an integral part of the work done by the Council to prepare the entire Church for a renewed apostolate in today's world. Deacons may rightfully be defined as *pioneers of the new civilization of love*, as John Paul II liked to say. I wish you an enjoyable and fruitful read.

Vatican City, July 31, 2017

# PART I
# A Special Encounter

*The poor you will always have with you . . .*
*(Mk 14:7)*

As I was leaving the Office of Papal Charities in the Vatican after having met with His Excellency Msgr. Konrad Krajewski, Pope Francis's papal almoner, this reflection came to mind: *Deacons and the healing of wounded families.*

The Synod certainly focused our attention on the problems of today's families, problems that often include separation, misunderstandings, and a lack of values. But what about the people who come from far away, disembarking in large numbers on the coast of our beautiful Italy? Are these not wounded families as well? These families have not been separated by personal misunderstandings or economic worsening but by the need to leave their home countries, where their dreams have been totally extinguished, to seek elsewhere hope with a different face and light, a name, a promise, a chance. And in order to do this, in order to take this journey, which for many will unfortunately be their last, fathers separate from their children, wives from their husbands. They depart, leaving behind a desert, unaware that they will most likely be swallowed up by an even more terrible desert of indifference, calculations, racism, and self-interests that have become all too personal. The *Instrumentum Laboris* from the Synod on the Family says that "today, migration is creating tragic consequences for masses of individuals and families, as if they were 'a surplus' in different populations and territories. These people legitimately seek a better future and, at times, a 're-birth' in those cases where they can no longer live in the place of their birth."[4]

When I received the unexpected gift of serving as a deacon for Pope Francis in the Sistine Chapel on the Feast of the Baptism of Jesus in 2014, I spoke to him about how deacons would like to do something dear to his heart. Without hesitation, he told me to speak his almoner. When I met him in his office that morning, the conversation transformed into a plea and even a warning: *Where are the deacons?*

He said this with deep respect but also with a lot of regret for the total absence of this ministry in the various "missions" that he carries out in the city of Rome. Almost every night, in the company of a Swiss Guard, he goes through the streets of Rome delivering nourishment (material nourishment as well as the nourishment of hope and consolation) to the capital's many homeless

---

4    XIV Ordinary General Assembly of the Synod of Bishops, *The Vocation and Mission of the Family in the Church and the Contemporary World*, Instrumentum Laboris (IL) (June 23, 2015), no. 24.

people. The showers and bathrooms located under the colonnades of St. Peter's Square were completed recently and are now accessible every day to dozens of people who can even receive a change of underwear. They are also working on opening another homeless shelter near Lungotevere in Sassia with the participation and help of St. Mother Teresa's sisters. He even went up against the law to get prefabricated buildings put up to house the hundreds of brothers who disembark on Italian shores and who have every right to immediate aid.

Msgr. Konrad's dream is to work with deacons to coordinate this enormous amount of work, which consists, not only of material assistance, food delivery, emergency funds, and clothing, but also a ministry of consolation, listening, support, and reliable points of reference. In preparation for the Synod on the Family, the *Instrumentum Laboris* urges us to give the gift of God's tenderness: "Tenderness means to give joyfully and, in turn, to stir in another person the joy of feeling loved. Tenderness is expressed in a particular way in looking at another's limitations in a loving way, especially when they clearly stand out. Dealing with delicacy and respect means attending to wounds and restoring hope in such a way as to revitalize trust in the other. . . . In this regard, Pope Francis invites everyone to reflect on his words: 'Do we have the courage to welcome with tenderness the difficulties and problems of those who are near to us, or do we prefer impersonal solutions, perhaps effective but devoid of the warmth of the Gospel? How much the world needs tenderness today! The patience of God, the closeness of God, the tenderness of God.'"[5]

The almoner was quite drastic in saying that the figure of the deacon, as we have been saying for years, cannot dedicate himself completely to celebrations. That is not his primary or original role.

He told me about a beautiful experience that a priest from a parish in the center of Rome is having with a soup kitchen that they open twice a day in their church. They could really use the concrete help of deacons in this service. Even though I totally shared his call, which originated only from the need to be as much of a presence as possible, to be the face and sign of Christ the Servant who spared nothing, I nevertheless felt very small when I recognized that what he was telling me was true: our precious and irreplaceable ministry needs to return to its roots, it needs to breathe in at the source, to draw near to others, to be a presence and humble service, not only in the nobility of the liturgy, where the poor should be the first ones taken to the altar anyway, but also in the humility of more humble and humiliating needs.

Listening to Msgr. Konrad, who leaves the Vatican every night to go out to the "peripheries," I thought of Jesus the Servant who, despite being the Son of God, chose as the last act of his earthly life to wash his friends' feet, which certainly were not clean or fragrant.

---

5    IL, Synod of Bishops on the Family (2015), no. 70.

After having celebrated the Jubilee of Mercy for deacons on May 29, 2016, do we now have the courage to lend an ear to this new kind of need? Will we have the evangelical simplicity needed to help those who are most vulnerable, the poorest, the ones who are furthest away, those who gratify us so little? We have the poor with us always—this is a true and terrible affirmation of the Gospel of Jesus. If the poor will always be here, then there must also always be deacons who have been ordained for service and not for glory.

The wounded families that we encounter in our ministry probably outnumber the idyllic families, the ones that seem healthy and look like the families we see in advertisements, leading us to believe something quite different from reality. Wounds worsen when nobody heals them, and they can become deadly. "Within the family are joys and trials, deep love and relationships which, at times, can be wounded. The family is truly the 'school of humanity' (cf. GS, no. 52), which is much needed today."[6]

The Word that was given to us on ordination day must burn in our hearts and become the need for giving, for presence, and for a serious warning for our daily lives and our formation. "The synod fathers repeatedly called for a thorough renewal of the Church's pastoral practice in light of the Gospel of the Family and for replacing

---

6    IL, Synod of Bishops on the Family (2015), no. 2.

its current emphasis on individuals. For this reason, the synod fathers repeatedly insisted on renewal in the training of priests, deacons, catechists and other pastoral workers with a greater involvement of families."[7]

It is a Word that heals wounds with the balm of consolation and hope. How many wounds torment families today? There may be too many to count. What about the families who have been devastated by oppressors who promise heaven and earth while loading children, mothers, and newborns on decrepit boats? What wounds do they have? The screams of children are wounds. The inconsolable cry of the mother, *Rachels* of the third millennium, challenges us in a serious way. The desperation on the tearless faces of fathers must wake us from our slumber. The river of tears mixed into the waters of our Mediterranean Sea shakes our conscience as deacons and minsters of service. On the journey from Jerusalem to Jericho . . . on the journey toward the depths of the wounds of the entire human family made up of brothers and sisters, may our diaconal ministry become aware of the wounds caused by the thieves of history. May it take the time to care for and even take over the burden of the needs of the wounded in order to take them toward the inn where Christ the Servant, making use of our hands, will tie on his apron and pass by to serve them one by one. "Many consider that the catechetical program for

7    IL, Synod of Bishops on the Family (2015), no. 87.

the family needs to be revised. In this regard, attention might be given to involving married couples in catechesis, especially with their children, in conjunction with priests, deacons and consecrated persons."[8]

May this become a reality!

---

8    IL, *The Vocation and Mission of the Family* (2015), no. 53.

# PART II

# The Diaconate in the Post-Conciliar Papal Magisterium

The Council marked the beginning of a new period for the diaconate, one characterized by an essential and arduous journey along two paths: on one hand, the normativization by the Holy See and episcopal conferences, and on the other, the awareness of communities that are opening up, even if slowly, to embrace this ministry.

Paul VI's papal document *Sacrum Diaconatus Ordinem*[9] includes the tasks outlined in conciliar texts, but also makes additions. For example, it adds guiding remote communities[10] to the deacon's responsibilities, a task that is not insignificant and that is capable of offering new perspectives on ministeriality and of opening up unexplored horizons to parish communities. Directives

---

9   Pope Paul VI, *Sacrum Diaconatus Ordinem* (June 18, 1967). After a brief introduction that refers to number 29 of *Lumen Gentium* (LG) and number 16 of *Ad Gentes* (AG), the document is divided into eight chapters: I. The Bishop's Responsibilities Toward the Permanent Diaconate; II. Young Deacons; III. Older Deacons; IV. The Incardination and Support of Deacons; V. Offices and Deacons; VI. The Spiritual Life and Duties of Deacons; VII. The Diaconate Among the Religious; VIII. Discipline in the Ordination of Deacons.

10  Ibid. *op. cit.*, V, 22, 10.

are also given for the formation of "young" and "adult" candidates, while other matters regarding the restoration of the diaconate are delegated to the episcopal conferences of each country. There are two observations of particular interest in this document.

The *first* has to do with the wife's consent. In paragraph 11, it is specified, in fact, that married men cannot be admitted to the diaconate "unless there is certainty not only about the wife's consent, but also about her blameless Christian life and those qualities which will neither impede nor bring dishonor on the husband's ministry." The *Code of Canon Law*[11] also states that a wife's consent is needed for the admission of a married candidate. However, the wife's consent, which is repeatedly stressed in all documents on the diaconate, is not merely formal consent; it is the wife's full, generous, and conscious acceptance that she exercises in deep and total agreement with her husband, so that the exercise of his ministry may translate each day into effective witness of the call he has received and authentic expression of the *diaconia* of Christ. In other words, the husband's diaconal vocation is not meant to be just accepted by the wife; it is a choice that the spouses must make *together* as their life's direction and plan. With her "yes," which is said in full awareness of her husband's ordination, she will also begin a new life of donation to the Church. This

---

11    *Code of Canon Law* (February 22, 1983), c. 1031 §2.

new life does not necessarily have to consist of particular engagements; it could involve simply guaranteeing her husband the family serenity and room for prayer that will help him in his ministry.

The *second* observation is the constant reference to the bond between bishop and deacon, which goes hand in hand with the reference to deacons Lawrence and Stephen, who are given as examples.

Lawrence's personal vicissitudes, which we have accounts of in ancient tradition dating back to the fourth century, are still of great inspiration to the diaconal ministry to this day. It is interesting to recount the particularly eloquent witness of St. Ambrose in *De Officiis*,[12] taken up again later by St. Augustine. Ambrose first talks at length about the encounter and dialogue between Lawrence and the pope. He then alludes to the distribution of the Church's goods to the poor. Finally, he mentions the gridiron, the instrument of torture by which his witness reaches its definitive fullness (*martyria*). The testimony of St. Ambrose is interesting for our reflection on diaconal identity[13] because through *martyria*, that is, through the full acceptance of the love or charity that becomes total self-sacrifice, the deacon gives supreme witness to Christ while persevering in the structural link that sacramentally binds him to the bishop and in the

---

12    Ambrose, *De Officiis*, 41, 205-207.

13    F. Moraglia, *St. Lawrence: Proto-Deacon of the Roman Church*, Speech Given to Deacons on the Occasion of the Jubilee in 2000.

service of an integral charity (thus, not only a human and social solidarity).[14] And the most evocative and interesting element that emerges from the exchange between Sixtus and Lawrence is this sacramental bond that ties the deacon to the bishop; it is a bond in which one (the deacon) is characterized as a "man of communion" precisely through the specific service to the other (the bishop). And in this service, which responds to the needs and urgencies of the Church, everything revolves around the altar, because everything in the Church finds its "source" and "summit" in the Eucharist.[15]

The communion and affection between bishop and deacon express a profoundly theological vision of the Church, overcoming concepts that lower or reduce the Church as Spouse to the merely political or sociological dimensions, equiparating her to one of the many human institutions. She is instead animated by the living and infinite reality of grace that constitutes the deep and inseparable link that binds her to Christ, *the One, True, Bishop, Priest and Deacon*. The association between bishop and deacon can be found in the New Testament

---

14  Ibid., *op. cit.*

15  Ambrose's testimony is particularly significant: "Lawrence . . . when he saw his bishop, Sixtus, led out to his martyrdom . . . he cried out to him in a loud voice: 'Where are you going Father, without your son? Where do you hasten to, holy Bishop, without your Deacon? You cannot offer sacrifice without a minister. . . . Do you not wish that he to whom you gave the Lord's blood and with whom you have shared the sacred mysteries should spill his own blood with you?"

(Ph 1:1 and 1 Tm 3:1-3), and the very close bond is attested to in both the *Traditio Apostolica*, which defines the grace given to the deacon at Ordination as *service to the bishop*, and the *Didascalia Apostolorum*, where the deacon is described as the *servant of the bishop and of the poor*. Finally, the strong structural relationship between deacon and bishop is clearly expressed in today's liturgy of Ordination. Unlike the Ordination of bishops and priests, the imposition of hands performed on the deacon is reserved to the ordaining bishop alone, precisely to highlight this deep and singular bond that links one to the other as a sign of the one and only *diaconia* of Christ.

Let us conclude this brief analysis of the contribution that *motu proprio* made to the profile of the permanent diaconate by pointing out that this document also gives us tools to nourish the spiritual lives of deacons: from the constant reading and studying of the Word of God and daily participation in the Eucharistic celebration, to regular participation in the Sacrament of Reconciliation and filial devotion to Mary. Lastly, explicit and heartfelt reference is made to the *permanent formation* of deacons.

In the period between the ecumenical council and *motu proprio*, Pope Paul VI gave two allocutions on the diaconate.[16] In both speeches, there is an exhortation to

---

16 One to the members of the First International Congress on the Diaconate (October 25, 1965), in *Nuovo Enchiridion sul Diaconato: Le fonti e i documenti ufficiali della Chiesa*, edited by E. Petrolino, LEV, Vatican City, 2016, p. 244.

implement the conciliar decisions so as to take a closer look at the mission of the deacon, whether single or married, and to work together to provide candidates with proper formation. At the same time, the pope pushes for the restoration of the diaconate in the Latin Church "to happen in charity," so that the deacon's presence may enrich, not only the ministerial order, but the entire community as well. The way Paul VI sees the deacon in the Church—united with "docility and affection" to his bishop—is very meaningful and underlines the spirit of service that must characterize the deacon who "is defined by service and who finds in service his assimilation to Christ, who—as Matthew says (20:28)—'came not to be served but to serve.'"[17] It is a commitment that requires great effort because the deacon is a sign of what the Church must do: be of service to the world.

The profile of the diaconal ministry is outlined even better in the document *Ad Pascendum*,[18] in which Paul VI reiterates that the deacon is the "animator of the service, or diaconia of the Church, among the local communities, and a sign or instrument of Christ the Lord himself."[19] The emphasis on the relationship between

---

17  To Members of the Study Commission on the Permanent Diaconate (February 24, 1967) in *Nuovo Enchiridion sul Diaconato: Le fonti e i documenti ufficiali della Chiesa*, edited by E. Petrolino, LEV, Vatican City, 2016, p. 245.

18  Pope Paul VI, *Ad Pascendum* (August 15, 1972).

19  Ibid., *op. cit.*, Introduction.

the deacon and the bishop and the exercise of charity that the bishop entrusts to the deacon are of particular importance here as well. Lastly, some additions are made regarding discipline: the rite of admission for candidates, which marks the beginning of the preparations for Ordination; the public assumption of "holy celibacy" before God and the Church, to be done before Ordination by candidates who are not married.

Paul VI addresses the responsibility of pastors to evangelize in the post-synodal Apostolic Exhortation *Evangelization in the Modern World.* "Deacons united with their bishops and whose assistants they are, by a communion which has its source in the sacrament of Orders and in the charity of the Church,"[20] are called to evangelization: to proclaim the Word of God with authority, to assemble the scattered People of God, to feed this People with the signs of the action of Christ, which are the sacraments, to set this People on the road to salvation, to maintain it in that unity of which we are, at different levels, active and living instruments, and unceasingly to keep this community gathered around Christ faithful to its deepest vocation.

John Paul II's pontificate did not leave us with any documents that comprehensively explain a systematic reflection on the diaconate, but this pope's great interest and pastoral care for the diaconal ministry stand out in

---

20  Pope Paul VI, *Evangelii Nuntiandi*, Post-Synodal Apostolic Exhortation on *Evangelization in the Modern World* (December 8, 1975), no. 68.

numerous speeches that he gave at meetings with deacons as well as in various apostolic exhortations and letters.[21] The speeches given to deacons from Italy[22] and the United States[23] are particularly significant.

In an excerpt from his speech to Italian deacons, the pope gives the theological coordinates of the deacon's identity with succinct clarity. "The Deacon, according to his grade, personifies Christ the Servant of the Father by participating in the threefold function of the Sacrament of Orders: a teacher insofar as he preaches and bears witness the Word of God; he sanctifies when he administers the Sacrament of Baptism, the Holy Eucharist and the

---

21 Cf. Apostolic Exhortation *Familiaris Consortio* (November 22, 1981); Apostolic Letter *Vicesimus Quintus Annus* (December 4, 1988); Post-Synodal Apostolic Exhortation *Christifideles Laici* (December 30, 1988); Apostolic Exhortation *Catechesi Tradendae* (December 30, 1988); Post-Synodal Apostolic Exhortation *Pastores Dabo Vobis* (March 25, 1992); Post-Synodal Apostolic Exhortation *Ecclesia in Africa* (September 14, 1995); Apostolic Letter *Dies Domini* (On Keeping the Lord's Day) (May 31, 1998); Post-Synodal Apostolic Exhortation on *The Encounter with the Living Jesus Christ: The Way to Conversion, Communion, and Solidarity in America* (January 22, 1999); Apostolic Letter *Novo Millennio Ineunte* (January 6, 2001); Post-Synodal Apostolic Exhortation *Ecclesia in Oceania* (November 22, 2001); Post-Synodal Apostolic Exhortation *Ecclesia in Europa* (June 28, 2003); Post-Synodal Apostolic Exhortation *Pastores Gregis* (October 16, 2003).

22 Pope John Paul II, Speech to Episcopal Delegates for the Permanent Diaconate and Deacons, promoted by the Italian Episcopal Conference (Rome, March 16, 1985).

23 Pope John Paul II, Speech Given to Deacons from the United States (September 19, 1987).

Sacramentals; he is a guide inasmuch as he animates the community or a section of ecclesial life."

Among the many aspects highlighted by the pope, one that is particularly effective is the affirmation that the service of the deacon is the Church's service sacramentalized. It is not just one of the many ministries, but it is truly meant to be a "driving force" for the diaconia of the Church. If we keep in mind the deep spiritual nature of this diaconia, then we can better appreciate the interrelation of the three areas of ministry traditionally associated with the diaconate, that is, the ministry of the word, the liturgy and charity. John Paul II also speaks about a "special witness" that deacons are called to give in society, precisely because their "secular occupation" gives them entry into the temporal sphere in a way that is normally not appropriate for other members of the clergy. At the same time, the married deacon contributes greatly to the transformation of family life by grace of the double sacramentality that characterizes his ministry. It is important to note how the involvement of the deacon's wife in her husband's public ministry in the Church is realized through the "nurturing and deepening of mutual, sacrificial love between husband and wife."

Reference to the Ordination Rite commits the deacon to what should be lifelong spiritual formation so that there is growth and perseverance in service that will truly edify the People of God.

The pope also talked about the diaconate during his Wednesday catechesis, where he addressed "the diaconate in the Church's ministerial and hierarchical communion, the deacon's functions in pastoral ministry, and features of diaconal spirituality."[24]

John Paul II, who holds the New Evangelization close to his heart, entrusts this "work" to the deacon's valuable contribution, which must be "marked by consistency and dedication, by courage and generosity, in the daily service of the liturgy, of the word and of charity."[25]

On the occasion of the Plenary Assembly of the Congregation for the Clergy,[26] which examined the *Instrumentum Laboris* with the intention of preparing a document concerning the life and ministry of permanent deacons similar to the one for priests, John Paul II gave a speech[27] that made an important contribution to a correct configuration of the diaconal ministry. Starting with conciliar doctrine, which then found its legal expression in the *Code of Canon Law*,[28] the pope hopes for careful theological research and prudent pastoral

---

24  Pope John Paul II gave these catecheses during audiences on October 6, 13, and 20 in 1993.

25  Pope John Paul II, *Angelus* for the Jubilee of Deacons (February 20, 2000).

26  Cf. Pope John Paul II, Speech on the Occasion of the Plenary Assembly for the Clergy (November 30, 1995).

27  Ibid., *op. cit.*

28  *Code of Canon Law*, c. 236, 1° and 2°; c. 276 §1, 1°-5°; c. 287 §1; c. 288; c. 1008; c. 1009 §1, §2; c. 1035 §1; c. 1301 §2, 3, 4.

sense, in light of the experience acquired, in view of the New Evangelization on the threshold of the third millennium, and summarizes everything that has to do with the life and ministry of deacons in a single word: *fidelity*. That means "fidelity to the Catholic tradition" as witnessed by the *lex orandi*; "fidelity to the magisterium; fidelity to the task of re-evangelization." All of this requires the careful promotion throughout the Church of "a sincere respect for the theological, liturgical, and canonical identity proper to the sacrament conferred on deacons." The pope then offers some points for reflection, keeping in mind the situation of deacons in the Universal Church.

Through the Sacrament of Orders, by the imposition of the bishop's hands and the specific prayer of consecration, the deacon receives a particular "configuration to Christ the Servant, the Head and Shepherd of the Church." Consequently, the deacon is no longer a layperson, nor can he be "reduced" to the lay state in the strict sense. This is why he is ordained; "to exercise a ministry of his own," which requires a "spiritual attitude of total dedication." This means that there are no "part-time" deacons, as they are "ministers of the Church" in all respects. The diaconate is not a *profession*, but a *mission*! It is with this in mind that we must examine the numerous unresolved problems associated with the need to make service to the Church compatible with other obligations (family, professional, social, etc.). To fulfill his mission in a full and authentic way, the deacon must have a "deep interior life" to nourish with an intense life of prayer that unites him with Christ and that allows him to find balance between his ministerial activities and his other professional, family, and social responsibilities.

John Paul II said that, at the time of its restoration, "some people saw the permanent diaconate as a bridge between pastors and the faithful." The terminology has great attractions and is still often used. The term *bridge*, however, also poses some important identity problems;[29] the image implies that there is a gap that must be bridged and that cannot be bridged unless there is a deacon. This distorts the whole meaning of the diaconal ministry. The idea of the diaconate as *medius ordo* (that is, "bridge") "might end up sanctioning and deepening, through that very function, the gap which it is supposed to fill."[30] On the other hand, the vision of Vatican II, particularly as set forth in *Gaudium et Spes*, is certainly more faithful to the truth and in the sign of communionality, as it talks about the "non-solution of continuity," or solidarity between the Church and the world, and about the diaconate as a splendid and special sign of this uninterrupted continuity.

---

29  See the excursus on the idea of *bridge* or *mediation* in the International Theological Commission's document, *From the Diakonia of Christ to the Diakonia of the Apostles* (2002), nos. 92-93.

30  Ibid., *op. cit.*, no. 93.

Even though he acknowledged that one of the main reasons for the Council's decision to restore the diaconate was "to provide for the scarcity of priests, as well as to assist them in many responsibilities not directly connected to their pastoral ministry," the pope noted, however, that those immediate and rather pragmatic reasons for restoring the permanent diaconate should not restrict our vision of this ministry today. He wrote: "The Holy Spirit, who has the leading role in the Church's life, was mysteriously working through these reasons connected with historical circumstances and pastoral perspectives in order to restore in the Church the complete picture of the ordained ministry, which is traditionally composed of bishops, priests, and deacons. Thus a revitalization of Christian communities was fostered, making them more like those founded by the apostles which flourished in the early centuries, always under the impulse of the Paraclete, as the Acts of the Apostles attest."[31]

These words suggest that the threefold ministry of bishops, priests, and deacons was a kind of engine that hummed in the hearts of Christian communities in the early Church. Doing without a third of that group for many centuries has made the Church's engine underpowered, and the pope looked forward to what might happen when full power was restored. It is notable that

---

31 Pope John Paul II, Catechesis audience, in *Nuovo Enchiridion sul Diaconato: Le fonti e i documenti ufficiali della Chiesa*, edited by E. Petrolino, LEV, Vatican City, 2016, p. 281.

the centuries when the diaconate was effectively absent have also been centuries when the laity became increasingly passive in the liturgy and increasingly neglected in terms of a formal apostolate. Thus, it is not groundless to observe that authentic flourishing of the diaconate helps and promotes the growth of the laity.

The publication of *Ratio Fundamentalis Institutionis Diaconorum Permanentium* (*Basic Norms for the Formation of Permanent Deacons*) and *Directorium Pro Ministerio et Vita Diaconorum Permanentium* (*Directory for the Ministry and Life of Permanent Deacons*)[32] was an important step in the clarification of the identity of deacons within the broader context of the entire ministry of the Church. These two documents, while retaining their own proper identities and specific juridical quality, were published together because they reflect and complete each other by virtue of their logical continuity.

These documents respond to the need felt by many to clarify and regulate the diversity of experiences taking place at the level of discernment and training or that of active ministry and ongoing formation. This need was also motivated by the fact that, following the reintroduction of the diaconate, many ecclesiastical

---

32  Congregation for the Clergy and the Congregation for Catholic Education, *Ratio Fundamentalis Institutionis Diaconorum Penmanentium* (*Basic Norms for the Formation of Permanent Deacons*) and *Directorium Pro Ministerio et Vita Diaconorum Permanentium* (*Directory for the Ministry and Life of Permanent Deacons*) (Vatican City, February 22, 1998).

regions experienced a "boom" in diaconal vocations;[33] a sign of the enthusiasm and hope that it created. These Vatican texts express the importance of the diaconate as a "sign," referring to deacons as "living icons of Christ the Servant"[34] within the Church. During a deacon's ordination, the bishop prays to God the Father that the newly-ordained may be "the image of your Son who did not come to be served but to serve."[35] Particularly since

---

33  Just look at the statistical data that we now have. The population of permanent deacons shows a significant evolutionary trend: an increase in 2015 of 14.4 percent compared to five years previously, from 39,564 to 45,255. The number of deacons is improving on every continent at a significant pace. In Oceania, where they do not yet reach 1 percent of the total, they have increased by 13.8 percent, amounting to 395. The figure is also improving in areas where their presence is quantitatively significant. In America and Europe, where about 98 percent of the total population of deacons is found, they have increased in the relevant period by 16.2 percent and 10.5 percent respectively.

"It is in the advanced industrialized countries of the North that the diaconate has developed particularly. Now that was not at all what the Council Fathers envisaged when they asked for a 'reactivation' of the permanent diaconate. They expected, rather, that there would be a rapid increase among the young Churches of Africa and Asia, where pastoral work relied on a large number of lay catechists. . . . What these statistics enable us to see is that there were two very different situations to be dealt with. On the one hand, after the Council, most of the Churches in Western Europe and North America were faced with a steep reduction in the numbers of priests, and had to undertake a major reorganization of ministries. On the other hand, the Churches that were mainly in former mission territories had long since adopted a structure that relied on the commitment of large numbers of laypeople, the catechists" (The Diaconate: Presentation of the Document of the International Theological Commission, *La Civiltà Cattolica*).

34  *Basic Norms*, no. 11

35  *Directory*, no. 38.

the Second Vatican Council, we have understood that the whole Church is called to a "spirituality of service" because it exists in the world to serve the salvation of the world. This perspective of the diaconate as a living "sign" for all those who are called to serve is what the documents express when they say: "So that the whole Church may better live out this spirituality of service, the Lord gives her a living and personal sign of his very being as servant."[36] It is crucial to keep this ecclesial context of the diaconate in mind.

These two documents maintain that the deacon participates in the "mystery of Christ the Servant,"[37] who gave his life as a "ransom for many" (Mt 20:28), and add that the deacon must be "a driving force for service."[38] Thus, it makes sense to repeat that deacons do not have a monopoly on service: it is the call of every disciple of Christ! But since this call is for everyone, it is very useful for everyone to have people who are specifically committed to a deep personal configuration to Christ the Servant by their side, people who can serve as *examples* and *signs* to remind everyone of what we must truly be. And seeing as the Church exists to love the world and to serve its salvation, we must extend our gaze to the needs of men, while always remembering that "the

---

36  *Basic Norms*, no. 11.

37  *Directory*, no. 57.

38  *Basic Norms*, no. 5.

object of Christ's diaconia is mankind."[39] These Vatican documents plug the deacon firmly into the agenda of *Gaudium et Spes* by asserting that the deacon "should be conversant with contemporary cultures and with the aspirations and problems of his times. In this context, indeed, he is called to be a living sign of Christ the Servant and to assume the Church's responsibility of 'reading the signs of the time and of interpreting them in the light of the Gospel.'"[40] Going back to John Paul II's profile of a deacon, through his engagement with family, work, school, etc., the deacon has a unique relationship with the aspirations and problems of his time. He sees the signs of the times close up every day, but, as an ordained minister of the Gospel, he is particularly called to read these signs and to interpret them in the light of the Gospel, so as to lead his Christian brothers and sisters who, by virtue of Baptism, are all charged with the same responsibility. Properly understood and lived, the diaconate should be a leaven for the apostolate of the laity.

---

39  *Directory*, no. 49.

40  *Directory*, no. 43.

The document *From the Diakonia of Christ to the Diakonia of the Apostles*[41] by the International Theological Commission (ITC) gives a thorough excursus on the past, while also explaining the positions that have developed in the post-conciliar period and encouraging further research. In this sense, the summary at the beginning of Chapter VII is meaningful for our work. It encourages us to examine how conciliar texts on the diaconate "were received and how they were later enlarged upon in the documents of the Magisterium, [to] take account of the fact that the restoration of the diaconate was accomplished very unevenly in the post-Conciliar period, and above all, [to] pay special attention to the doctrinal fluctuations which have closely shadowed the various pastoral suggestions." After reminding us that "today there are numerous very different aspects which require an effort at doctrinal clarification[,] this chapter attempt[s] to contribute to these efforts at clarification . . . [by] first pinpoint[ing] the roots and reasons which make the theological and ecclesial identity of the diaconate (both

---

41   As it is written in the foreword, this document is the product of two subcommissions and a revision by the ITC itself during its plenary sessions. It is a significant expression of the role of theologians in the Church, which is "to pursue in a particular way an ever deeper understanding of the Word of God found in the inspired Scriptures and handed on by the living Tradition of the Church. He does this in communion with the Magisterium which has been charged with the responsibility of preserving the deposit of faith" (cf. Congregation for the Doctrine of Faith, *On the Ecclesial Vocation of the Theologian* [1990], no. 6).

permanent and transitory) into a real *quaestio disputata* in certain respects" and then "outlin[ing] a theology of the diaconal ministry which may serve as a firm common basis to inspire the fruitful re-creation of the diaconate in Christian communities." This renewal must be carried out in continuity with Tradition. Chapter II of the document helps us along this path by rebuilding a sense of heritage.

After examining Paul VI's Motu Proprio *Ad Pascendum*, the document addresses the sacramentality of the permanent diaconate in relation to what is expressed in conciliar texts and affirms that "the most reliable doctrine and that most in accord with ecclesial practice is that which holds that the diaconate is a sacrament. If its sacramentality were denied the diaconate would simply represent a form of ministry rooted in baptism; it would take on a purely functional character, and the Church would possess a wide faculty of decision-making with regard to restoring or suppressing it, and to its specific configuration."[42]

The document scrutinizes the complexity of an ecclesial reality that, in some respects, does not seem to have fully understood the spirit of the Council but that takes off toward the necessary and never-ending path on which the community of believers matures its sense of

---

42   ITC, *From the Diakonia of Christ to the Diakonia of the Apostles*, Ch. VII, Sect. II.

belonging to Christ and, from that awareness, its own communional dimension.[43]

The entire sacrament of Holy Orders, and in particular the diaconate, is valuable for the good of the entire Church when it has a *proprium* that is not fragmented into single directions (liturgy, charity, pastoral work) but harmonized by a united outlook on the various fields of effective implementation of ecclesial action and that makes use of the different structuring elements of the action of Christian fraternity. It is within this framework of unity that the sacramentality of the diaconate must be understood. The three fundamental expressions of the Church's ministry—episcopate, presbyterate, and diaconate—cannot be reduced and cannot substitute one another. They act in organic unity so that ecclesial fraternity can be edified in the Body of Christ and to fulfill the mission received from him. After illustrating the characterizations of the episcopate and presbyterate, the document focuses on the ministry of the deacon. It affirms that, starting with the Eucharist, which is presided over by the bishop or priest, the deacon is responsible for implementing or taking care of the realization

---

43 A passage from the document reads: "The specific way the diaconate is exercised in different surroundings will also help to define its ministerial identity, modifying if necessary an ecclesial framework in which its proper connection with the ministry of the bishop hardly appears and in which the figure of the priest is identified with the totality of the ministerial functions. The living consciousness that the Church is 'communion' will contribute to this development" (Ch. VII, Sect. IV, 2).

of ecclesial action (directly or through the charisms and ministries of others) in its various spheres (first evangelization, education of the Christian, edification of ecclesial fraternity, effective presence in society) as an ordained collaborator of the episcopal and presbyteral orders.

The document often speaks about the permanent diaconate as a "form" to recover and reinstate today in the Church, so that "over and above all the questions raised by the diaconate, it is good to recall that ever since Vatican II the active presence of this ministry in the life of the Church has aroused, in memory of the example of Christ, a more vivid awareness of the value of service for Christian life."[44]

Pope Benedict XVI certainly left us with some profound words on this subject,[45] and it is enlightening that in *Deus Caritas Est*[46] he stressed that "the Church cannot neglect the service of charity any more than she can neglect the Sacraments and the Word. . . . Love for widows and orphans, prisoners, and the sick and needy of every kind, is as essential to her as the ministry of the

---

44  *From the Diakonia of Christ to the Diakonia of the Apostles*, Ch. VII, Sect. V.

45  In the post-synodal Apostolic Exhortation *Sacramentum Caritatis* (February 22, 2007), nos. 26, 39, 51, 53, 61, 75, and 94; Speech Given to Deacons in Brazil (May 12, 2007); Audience with the Clergy of the Rome Diocese (February 8, 2008).

46  Pope Benedict XVI, Encyclical Letter *Deus Caritas Est* (Vatican City, December 25, 2005).

sacraments and preaching of the Gospel."[47] The pope affirms that, with the choice of "the seven" and their absolutely concrete, yet at the same time spiritual service, "diaconia became part of the fundamental structure of the Church."[48] And in his speech to Roman deacons,[49] Pope Benedict XVI pointed out the new forms of poverty that characterize our times: many people have lost the meaning of life or face spiritual and cultural poverty. Even in liturgical service, the deacon should address these poverties in order to bring all the poor to Christ's altar, but we should not spiritualize the meaning of poverty so much that we forget the deacon's call to serve the poor *materially* with an effective love. The pope points out that it is not enough to proclaim the faith with words alone, but that it is necessary to back up the proclamation of the Gospel with a practical witness of charity. Only a powerful reaffirmation of the primacy of the diaconal ministry of charity will guarantee acceptance and a long future for the restored diaconate. Otherwise, it could suffer the same fate as the diaconate in the early Church, getting trapped between the fear of posing a threat to the identity of priests and the concerns of the laity regarding new forms of clericalism. This must be kept in mind when searching for suitable

---

47   Ibid., *op. cit.*, no. 22.

48   Ibid., *op. cit.*, no. 21.

49   Pope Benedict XVI, Speech to the Permanent Deacons of Rome (February 18, 2006).

means of promotion and discernment of the diaconate and for valid paths of formation of future deacons.

Pope Benedict hopes "that despite the differing situations, charity will continue in every age and every diocese to be a fundamental as well as a key dimension for the commitment of deacons, although not the only one. We see this in the primitive Church where the seven deacons were elected precisely to enable the Apostles to devote themselves to prayer, the liturgy and preaching. Even if Stephen later found he was required to preach to Hellenists and to Greek-speaking Jews, the field of preaching was in this way extended. He was conditioned, we can say, by the cultural situations in which he had a voice in order to make the Word of God present in this field in such a way as also to extend as far as possible the universality of Christian witness. Thus, he opened the door to St. Paul, who was a witness to his stoning and subsequently, in a certain sense, his successor in the universalization of the Word of God."[50]

The Second Vatican Council affirmed that the bishop has the fullness of the Sacrament of Orders and that he is the primary celebrant of the Eucharist among

---

50    Pope Benedict XVI, Meeting with the Parish Priests and the Clergy of the Diocese of Rome (February 7, 2008).

his people.[51] Conciliar teaching on the permanent diaconate must be understood within the overall structuring of the Church around the Eucharist, the source and summit of the whole Christian life[52] and the overall celebration of the Eucharist around the bishop. In this ministerial connotation of the whole Church, the deacon is fundamentally tied to the Eucharist and to the bishop. The liturgy is indeed "the summit toward which the activity of the Church is directed" and "the font from which all her power flows."[53] Pope Benedict XVI (then Cardinal Ratzinger) neatly summarized the Vatican II teaching on this topic when he said, "[The Church's] worship service is her constitution, for by her very nature she is service of God and therefore service of men, the service that transforms the world."[54] He then says that what deacons do in the liturgy and how they relate to the other ministries will be symbolic of their activity and relationships in the world at large.

"The celebration of the Eucharist is a paradigm for the interrelationship of various ministries in the Church.

---

51    *Sacrosanctum Concilium* (SC), no. 41: "The pre-eminent manifestation of the Church consists in the full active participation of all God's holy people in these liturgical celebrations, especially in the same eucharist, in a single prayer, at one altar, at which there presides the bishop surrounded by his college of priests and by his ministers [deacons]."

52    Ibid., *op. cit.*, no. 10.

53    Ibid., *op. cit.*, no. 10.

54    J. Ratzinger, *Church, Ecumenism, and Politics: New Endeavors in Ecclesiology* (Cinesello Balsamo, Italy: Edizioni Paoline, 1987).

It is among other things, a kind of 'dress rehearsal' for life."[55]

If service at the table, which is rendered first to brothers then to all the poor, is derived by natural sacramental expansion from the diaconia of the Eucharist, then from *diaconia verbi*[56] comes a true ministry of the Word that finds its biblical source and precise ecclesial identity in the evangelization of the least and the marginalized. Therefore, it is fundamental to the ordained diaconia to recognize the deacon's concrete aptitude to be the animator of the service of the Word, not only in the liturgy and charity, but also in the Christian community he belongs to.

To conclude this lengthy overview, I would like to focus on a few new elements that were introduced by Benedict XVI in his Motu Proprio *Omnium in Mentem*

---

55  Hanover Report by the Anglican-Lutheran International Commission (London, Anglican Commission Publications, 1996); *The Diaconate as Ecumenical Opportunity*, no. 22.

56  The *Instrumentum Laboris* from the XII Synod of Bishops on *The Word of God in the Life and Mission of the Church* (June 12, 2008) states in number 49: "Knowledge of and familiarity with the Word of God is also of prime importance for priests and deacons in their calling to the ministry of evangelization. The Second Vatican Council states that, by necessity, all the clergy, primarily priests and deacons, ought to have continual contact with the Scriptures, though assiduous reading and attentive study of the sacred texts, so as not to become idle preachers of the Word of God, hearing the Word only with their ears while not hearing it with their hearts (cf. DV 25; PO 4). In keeping with this conciliar teaching, canon law speaks of the ministry of the Word of God entrusted to priests and deacons as collaborators of the Bishop."

(October 26, 2009) to define the Sacrament of Holy Orders and the identity of the diaconate. These elements also make public a change in the *Catechism of the Catholic Church* introduced by John Paul II in 1998 and reformulate canon 1008 and canon 1009 of the *Code of Canon Law* (CIC) in a way that is consistent with the doctrinal decision made by his predecessor.

On the topic of the Sacrament of Holy Orders, the *Catechism* reads: "This sacrament configures the recipient to Christ by a special grace of the Holy Spirit, so that he may serve as Christ's instrument for his Church. By ordination one is enabled to act as a representative of Christ, Head of the Church, in his triple office of priest, prophet, and king."[57] As you can see, after a general statement on the specific configuration to Christ of those who receive this sacrament, the text points out a feature that is unique to the three degrees of Holy Orders and that distinguishes holy ministers from those who are only baptized: the ability to act as Christ, Head of the Church.

Following the modification introduced by John Paul II and promulgated by Benedict XVI, this code of the CIC was rewritten to read: "Those who are constituted in the order of the episcopate or the presbyterate receive the mission and capacity to act in the person of Christ the Head, whereas deacons are empowered to serve the

---

57    *Catechism of the Catholic Church*, no. 1581.

People of God in the ministries of the liturgy, the word and charity."[58]

The pope's document seems determined to offer new elements to help clarify the nature of the Sacrament of the Holy Orders and to better define the identity of the diaconate.

It was common opinion that the Second Vatican Council and post-conciliar Magisterium were clear and decisive (a) in reiterating the unity of the Sacrament of Holy Orders, distinct in its three degrees: episcopate, presbyterate, and diaconate; (b) in affirming that its specific element is to preside over the community in the name of Christ the Head; and (c) in attesting to the sacramental dimension of the diaconate.

The modifications introduced by the Motu Proprio *Omnium in Mentem* seem to revolve around how the expression "presiding in the name of Christ the Head" is used. Traditionally, this expression defined a directional function, and it was used in this sense in the *Catechism* and *Code of Canon Law*: The Sacrament of Holy Orders, it in its three degrees, conferred an office of presidency in the exercise of the *tria munera* upon those who received it.

With a more restricted meaning, "presiding in the name of Christ the Head" referred to the power to preside over the celebration of the Eucharist, which

---

58   *Code of Canon Law*, can. 1009 § 3.

only falls to the two degrees of the episcopate and the presbyterate.

The modifications that were introduced make it look as though the Papal Magisterium intends to favor the second meaning, excluding deacons from this role.

Consequently, however, this choice raises some doubts:

- It becomes more problematic to clearly identify the *proprium* of the Sacrament of Holy Orders. The only description that can be attributed to the three degrees in the modified text is this: "This sacrament configures the recipient to Christ by a special grace of the Holy Spirit, so that he may serve as Christ's instrument for his Church." Being "Christ's instrument for his Church" cannot be considered the specific task of those who have received the Sacrament of Holy Orders because it is a task that belongs to the community as a whole and to each baptized person individually.

- Reserving the function of presiding over the community in the name of Christ the Head to bishops and priests creates separation within the Sacrament of Holy Orders. For example, what about when a deacon celebrates the Sacrament of Baptism or coordinates charitable activities in the diocese on behalf of the bishop? Is he not presiding over the community in the name of Christ the Head? The modifications introduced highlight the differences that separate the diaconate from the presbyterate and the episcopate. This could give fresh impetus to those who deny the sacramental dimension of the diaconate and who propose that deacons be thought of as men who are simply baptized and entrusted with particular ministries.

- The recent modifications established by the Papal Magisterium affirm a role of service for deacons as an alternative to presiding in the name of Christ the Head: "Deacons are empowered to serve the People of God in the ministries of the liturgy, the word and charity."[59] Within the one Sacrament of Holy Orders, how can we make reference to Christ the Head for bishops and priests, and yet, only refer to Christ the Servant for deacons?

The International Theological Commission writes about this in the abovementioned document: "Difficulties arise, not because of the central importance of the notion of service for every ordained minister, but because this is made the specific criterion of the diaconal ministry. Could 'headship' and 'service' in the representation

---

59 Pope Benedict XVI, Apostolic Letter Motu Proprio *Omnium in Mentem* (October 26, 2009), art. 2.

of Christ be separated so as to make each of the two a principle of specific differentiation? Christ the Lord is at the same time the supreme Servant and the servant of all. The ministries of the bishop and the priest, precisely in their function of presiding and of representing Christ the Head, Shepherd and Spouse of his Church, also render Christ the Servant visible, and require to be exercised as services. This is why it would seem problematic to aim to distinguish the diaconate through its exclusive representation of Christ as Servant."[60]

Keep in mind, however, that despite the latest modifications, the *Catechism* still confirms the representation of Christ the Head for the Sacrament of Holy Orders as a whole: "In the ecclesial service of the ordained minister, it is Christ himself who is present to his Church as Head of his Body, Shepherd of his flock, high priest of the redemptive sacrifice, Teacher of Truth."[61]

One does not have to be an expert in canon law to see how difficult it is employ the schematic and concise language used in legal standards to summarize theological issues of such complexity; issues which really require a different kind of language and methodology.

---

60  *From the Diakonia of Christ to the Diakonia of the Apostles*, Ch. VII, Sect. II, 4.

61  *Catechism of the Catholic Church*, no. 1548.

# The Diaconate in the Context of Ecumenism

The ecumenical context of the diaconal ministry surely plays an important part in the post-conciliar Magisterium. The mission of the deacon is also ecumenical hope in the Church because this ministry prophetically gives new perspectives on the concrete ecclesial reality.

The deacon's service is a service for ecumenism which may be less tangible and gratifying than other offices, but which is certainly no less engaging than the sacramental diaconia that is correctly understood and lived in the triple dimension of the Word, the Altar, and the Poor. It is a service for the cause of the unity of Christians, a cause that concerns the entire world, which longs for unity, peace, justice, and salvation.

This ministry is, in fact, called to propose—by example and with theological study—the absolute priority of service in every ministry.

Furthermore, "in recent ecumenical reflection on the diaconate . . . the ministry of deacons has been seen as that of a go-between, a bridge, an envoy, whose special ministry is to take the message, meaning and values of the liturgy, as a key expression of the gospel, into the heart of the world, and by the same token, to bring the needs and cares of the world into the heart of the Church's worship and fellowship. Deacons have been seen as those who, grounded in the teaching and worship of the Body of Christ, carry the good news, in word and sacrament, and through compassionate service, to those whom Christ came to seek and to save."[62]

While this wonderful description of the diaconate testifies to the growing approval that the diaconate has met over time at the ecumenical level, it also helps us understand that deacons are actually "signs" for the Church of all that it should do. It would be misleading, in fact, to describe and evaluate the diaconate only in functional terms. This is why today ecumenism is an important setting for the renewal of the diaconate.

So far, only one ecumenically agreed statement has been produced specifically on the diaconate, namely the so-called Hanover Report of the Anglican-Lutheran International Commission, entitled *The Diaconate as Ecumenical Opportunity*.[63] This valuable text reinforces the point just made, that is, that "the integration of worship and service remains a concern for the various diaconal ministries of the Church. . . . Diaconal ministry typically seeks, not only to mediate the service of the Church to specific needs, but also to interpret those needs to the Church. The 'go-between' role of diaconal

---

62 *For such a time as this: A renewed diaconate in the Church of England.* "A Report to the General Synod of the Church of England of a Working Party of the House of Bishops" (London: Church House Publishing, 2001).

63 The Hanover Report, *op. cit.*, in order no. 28, 51, 22.

ministry thus operates in both directions: from the Church to the needs, hopes, and concerns of persons in and beyond the Church; and from those needs, hopes, and concerns to the Church."[64]

This requires a "new incarnation" of diaconia in the most troubled places of our time. It requires careful listening to the "cry of the poor" in the most diverse situations of our existence, situations that often cannot be immediately assimilated to the common experience because they derive from unresolved conflicts, ethnic prejudices, and socioeconomic and political conditions that have given way to new kinds of poverty, new questions of meaning, and new challenges for our capacity for dialogue and change. The ecumenical exchange of ideas and experiences is a fundamental place for different forms of ministerial diaconia to meet, understand, and enrich one another in order to proclaim the Gospel of hope and peace to all men: a proclamation that can become concrete and liberating "service" anywhere and for anyone.[65]

The reintroduction of the permanent diaconate should definitely be seen, in light of the post-conciliar Magisterium, as an integral part of the work done by the Council to prepare the whole Church for a renewed apostolate in today's world.

---

64  Ibid., op. cit., no. 28, no. 51.

65  W. Kasper, *Leadership in the Church: How Traditional Roles Can Serve the Christian Church Today*, tr. Brian McNeil (New York, 2003).

# PART III

# The Diaconate in the Thought of Pope Francis

More than four years have passed since the historic and revolutionary resignation of Benedict XVI (announced on February 11, 2013) and the election of Pope Francis (March 13, 2013), a period which transformed the deepest expression of the Church at its roots.

We must say that it is still too soon to understand what Francis thinks about the diaconal ministry,[66] although it must be said that the pope's style is one of a true deacon of joy, simplicity, and evangelical poverty. Here I will try to interpret his thought on the diaconate, a thought that is significantly present in some of the speeches he gave as cardinal in the Diocese of Buenos Aires and in his Papal Magisterium, even if he was not speaking specifically about deacons.

---

66 "Another thing that often happens, Francis said in his off-the-cuff address to representatives of Italian diocesan broadcasters, is that 'when there is a lay person who does a good job and is committed, their parish priest goes to the local bishop—and this happened to me in Buenos Aires—and says: "Why don't we make him a deacon?" This is a mistake: if we have a good lay person, let him carry on being just that,' the pope stressed" (Pope Francis, Audience with Italian television and radio network, Corallo Association [March 22, 2014], English translation from La Stampa).

# I. The Diaconal Theology of Simplicity

There are traits of a seemingly unprecedented and disruptive break with tradition[67] in the Magisterium of the Argentinian pope, the first being his choice of language. Since he gives priority and special attention to being understood by normal people, he prefers the simplicity and essentiality of the Gospel message over great theological and doctrinal discourse and favors the invitation to live and witness a coherent experience of faith over making effort to win over the intelligentsia with acceptable rationality.

For decades, there have been complaints about how many ecclesial documents there are, maybe even too many. Sure, they are well-structured from a theological and editorial point of view. They are undoubtedly beautiful and interesting, but often they are also difficult and are read by very few people. They are also repetitive, as they are composed of quotations from previous documents. We cannot hide the fact that most of the faithful have not even had access to these documents. They have not been interested in them, nor have they felt like the documents pertain to them. Even if they have had access to these documents, we cannot deny that they

---

67 Cf. The Words of Pope Francis, *Morning Homilies*, vol. 1-8, LEV, Vatican City, 2013-2017.

were written in a language that essentially can only be used by a select few.

Something then has changed for good. In the Encyclical *Lumen Fidei* and in the Apostolic Exhortation *Evangelii Gaudium*, it is revealed that the Father's mercy, tenderness, and love toward his creatures and the gift of faith are not precious treasures to be jealously guarded, but to be spread in a commitment of brotherhood, peace, and hope. The images of the Church as a field hospital that heals wounds of humanity and the reality of the geographical and, more importantly, human peripheries as a symbol of the Incarnation do not seem like calls or desires, but the sign of a Christianity that wants to save man in his ferial and ordinary dimension by opposing a culture of consumption, oppression, and violence. "The 'peripheries' of the basic communities of deacons, religious men and women, and the laity are the guarantee of a place for communion, participation, socialization, authentic evangelization, and catechesis."[68] So, not only must life must be protected from its beginning and in its natural conclusion, but through everything in between, in the fulfillment of men and women in their freedom and dignity.

---

68    At the Fifth CELAM Conference, *Aparecida* (May 30, 2007).

# II. Diaconal Language

There is a time and place for the incarnation of the missionary order to "go forth" that resonates throughout the Gospel for those who live in the following of Christ: the time is in the *today* of our personal and social experience, and the place is *here* in our every action and plan. But now, with a heartfelt and insistent plea, Pope Francis urges us to bring the Good News of the Kingdom to the "outskirts of existence," to the places where—as he has said on many occasions—"there is suffering, bloodshed, blindness that longs for sight, and prisoners in thrall to many evil masters,"[69] places inhabited by all those marked by "physical and . . . intellectual poverty,"[70] by "those who seem farthest away, most indifferent,"[71] places where "God is absent."[72] The outskirts, however, must not be "predefined" by our prejudice, as if we were taking salvation to "lost islands." While the outskirts are often ignored by the dynamics of political power and excluded by large economic interests, they

---

69   Pope Francis, Homily at Chrism Mass (March 28, 2013).

70   Pope Francis, Address to Participants in the Ecclesial Convention of the Diocese of Rome (June 17, 2013).

71   Pope Francis, Homily on the Occasion of the Twenty-Eighth World Youth Day (July 28, 2013).

72   Pope Francis, Pastoral Visit to Assisi, Meeting with the Clergy, Consecrated People, and Members of Diocesan Pastoral Councils (October 4, 2013).

nevertheless remain places of encounter and fraternity that are filled with expectations and needs but that are also rich in dreams and resources. The "outskirts" are the new frontier for proclamation and, at the same time, a true school of fruitful listening and generous availability. In the often senseless and vain restlessness of big cities, the outskirts remain surprisingly aware of their limits and willing to learn from other experiences that might enrich them. People who live there generally have to make do with the essentials, each and every day, and cannot afford the luxuries of excess and worldly pleasures. The outskirts of existence remain anchored to reality, to joys and hopes, and to the anxieties and fears they experience in their daily lives. Here, a different ecclesial experience really becomes possible, one that is characterized by an essential return to a more spiritual dimension: true and deep spirituality does not put formal aspects first; it goes straight to the essentials. The "outskirts of existence" that Pope Francis is talking about, therefore, do not coincide *tout court* with the geographical areas that often develop in repetitive and impersonal patterns around large urban centers. Rather, they are places of "suffering" and "development" where life and faith can be brought back and rediscovered in their indissoluble bond through pastoral work that is intimately connected to real experience.

Before we can understand, we must get on the same wavelength as our brothers, feeling *cum corde* with them and their deepest expectations for liberation, growth, sharing, and salvation. Yes, here it is possible to build and be part of a different Church. A Church that is, first of all, made up of people, where the community becomes the vital core and where rituals are no longer at the center of attention. A Church characterized by its mercy and its ability to listen from the heart in the dimensions and on the levels of those who are in distress, grief, pain, and misery. Finally, we are facing another break, one that will bring the community, the People of God, and diaconia back to the center as the Kingdom's only purpose in place of the curia, rubrics, or luxurious vestments; while these things fulfill a role in the ecclesial structure, if they are overestimated and preponderant, they increase—rather than decrease—gaps and distances, inexorably distancing the credibility of the proclamation from ordinary people, especially from the poor and the least.

# III. A Diaconal Reading of the Apostolic Exhortation *Evangelii Gaudium*

The Apostolic Exhortation *Evangelii Gaudium* (*On the Proclamation of the Gospel in Today's World*) published on November 24, 2013, makes an initial impression for what it lacks, in my opinion, intentionally. Those who are looking for completeness of theological argumentation, perfect proportion of parts, or precise balance of quotations will be let down. Instead, they will be blown away by a healthy and beneficial explosion through which a series of powerful evangelical materials push the entire Church to renew her missionary conscience, to begin a process of reformation, and to introduce into the lives of believers the joy of proclamation, toward a permanent state of mission. Mission thus becomes the paradigm of all evangelization: "Personal conversion arouses the ability to submit everything to the service of the establishment of the Kingdom of life. Bishops, priests, permanent deacons, consecrated persons, lay persons, are all called to take up an attitude of permanent pastoral conversion, which implies listening with attention and discernment 'to what the Spirit is saying to the churches' (Rev 2:29) through the signs of the times where God manifests Himself. May we be fascinated, attracted, seized by the love of Christ so we may say with St. Paul, 'I should be punished if I did not preach it'! May the Mother of the Lord, who, in particular, knew heaviness of heart, accompany and sustain us in our daily trials, and may she obtain for us the grace of evangelical boldness, zeal, and constancy of apostolic mission."[73]

---

73   Speech given at the first meeting of the Council of Priests, Buenos Aires (April 15, 2008).

The pope's words also contribute to guiding the processes of self-awareness and evolution of the ordained diaconia. I indeed believe that reflecting on the diaconate and on the reception of the results of the council concerning the diaconate in our Churches will allow us to expand the horizons of the entire life and mission of the Church in our time. The deacon is the witness and servant of the mission, he is a minister of a Church that is called—as John Paul II liked to say—to find herself outside of herself.

The intentionality of *Evangelii Gaudium* is seen less in its attention toward writing style and effective rhetorical form than in the personal and intimately sincere way its author, Pope Francis, expresses himself. He writes: "My mission of being in the heart of the people is not just a part of my life or a badge I can take off; it is not an 'extra' or just another moment in life. Instead, it is something I cannot uproot from my being without destroying my very self. I am a mission on this earth; that is the reason why I am here in this world."[74] Even at the cost of feeling "disoriented: it is like being plunged into the deep and not knowing what we will find. I myself have frequently experienced this."[75]

Not expecting to make a comprehensive list, and venturing to choose among the numerous suggestions,

---

74  EG, no. 273.
75  EG, no. 280.

I have identified some points from the document that are particularly original and relevant to the diaconate and that may be of service to our ministry: (a) the joy of proclamation, (b) the priority of the Gospel, (c) the need for mission, and (d) the preferential option for the poor.

## A) The Joy of Proclamation

"The joy of the gospel fills the hearts and lives of all who encounter Jesus. Those who accept his offer of salvation are set free from sin, sorrow, inner emptiness and loneliness. With Christ joy is constantly born anew."[76] The "passions" that sometimes, sadly, permeate the frantic search for human and social self-affirmation find denial and upheaval in scriptural texts, but not always in an evangelical and coherent lifestyle. There are Christians, and unfortunately even deacons, who know more about Lent than Easter, more about self-pity than fraternal impetus, more about retreat and resignation than joyful witness of the benefits received. As we all know, deacons are traditionally assigned the task of singing the *Exsultet* during the Easter Vigil. It opens with a hymn to the joy of Easter, which the deacon proclaims to three categories that are called to give praise to the Risen One: the *host of angels*, the first witnesses to the Resurrection; the *Earth*,

---

76    EG, no. 1.

liberated from the darkness of sin; and *mother Church*, represented by the assembly gathered in the temple. This is why, liturgically speaking, the joyful *Exsultet* is the most visible office of the diaconal ministry, as well as an example of the "modus" that should animate the evangelizing mission of every disciple.

The joy of the faith is not subject to the countless conditions of objects that transform into needs and needs that transform into desires of the globalized civilization. It lives even in inhospitable contexts, and this extraordinary force, which seems contradictory and, therefore, remains incomprehensible to the mental categories of the world, is actually connatural and proper to the joy of the faith because the encounter with God's love redeems the conscience from all isolation and solitude and breaks down the walls of self-referentiality and of self-reliance.

## B) The Priority of the Gospel

The urgency of the mission imposes the priority of the Gospel. As deacons, we all received the Book of the Gospels from the bishop at Ordination. The deacon, who is a Servant of the Gospel by sacramental grace, holds up and carries the Holy Book so that it may be given to the faithful. The deacon prepares the gift of the Gospel; better yet, he performs all of the actions that are prerequisites to the proclamation of the Gospel by the priest, thereby serving the Word through *praeparatio*

*Evangelii.* What does preparing for the Gospel mean? It means helping man complete his journey toward an encounter with Christ, just as the deacon Philip did (cf. Acts 8:26). This implies total adherence to the Master, the constant pursuit of conformation to him and to the diaconal model embodied by him, and the endless desire to "walk through the deserts of humanity."[77] We cannot be reductively "obsessed with the disjointed transmission of a multitude of doctrines to be insistently imposed,"[78] nor identify the message with its secondary aspects "which, important as they are, do not in and of themselves convey the heart of Christ's message."[79]

## C) The Need for Mission

Throughout the text, there is a dramatic and enthusiastic dimension regarding mission that expresses the identity of the Church and the personal realization of the believer. "The new evangelization calls for personal involvement on the part of each of the baptized."[80] There is also the important message: "Jesus Christ loves you; he gave his life to save you; and now he is living

---

77    Pope Francis, Homily at the Mass for the Closing of the Fourteenth Ordinary General Assembly of the Synod of Bishops (October 25, 2015).

78    EG, no. 35.

79    EG, no. 34.

80    EG, no. 120.

at your side every day to enlighten, strengthen and free you."[81] The way of beauty and the way of the Word require the proclamation of the *kerygma* to "express God's saving love which precedes any moral and religious obligation on our part; it should not impose the truth but appeal to freedom; it should be marked by joy, encouragement, liveliness and a harmonious balance which will not reduce preaching to a few doctrines which are at times more philosophical than evangelical."[82] Once again, it is the *presentation of the Gospel Book* during the ordination of the deacon that shows us the clear link between the place that the new deacon will occupy in the Church and the way to exercise his ministry. Proclaim the Gospel and practice what it teaches: it is in these dynamic terms that the Church entrusts the newly ordained with the *diaconia* of the Word. Only prolonged and varied practice will reveal the deep meaning of a word proclaimed by a person who is sacramentally ordained but who, nevertheless, is not removed from his family, his cultural environment, or his profane work.

---

81 EG, no. 164.

82 EG, no. 165.

# D) The Preferential Option for the Poor

A *Church which is poor and for the poor*[83] and so, a Church that is truly *diaconal*: this is the wish that has accompanied the ministry of Pope Francis since the beginning. And it is a wish that continually serves as a guiding principle for the spiritual and ecclesial renewal that is outlined so effectively in *Evangelii Gaudium*: to rediscover in the joy of the Gospel the true richness that the Church is called to live and witness. Latin American tradition relative to the preferential option for the poor and the poor Church is fully reflected in the papal exhortation. One can sense the deep continuity created through the Magisterium and practices of the Churches on that continent—this continent—over the last fifty years, as well as the struggles, conflicts, and progress in theology and pastoral practices. Purification from the ideological waste and laziness allows for surprising clarity in the denunciation of "the absolute autonomy of markets and financial speculation."[84] "We can no longer trust in the unseen forces and the invisible hand of the market,"[85] unless we plan on no longer speaking about personal and collective ethics, solidarity, the distribution of goods, work, and the dignity of the weak. The need for the option for

---

83 The expression was first used in the speech to media representatives by Pope Francis on March 16, 2013. Full text available at *www.vatican.va*.

84 EG, no. 202.

85 EG, no. 204.

the poor is already too strong, and not for purely socio-logical reasons, but rather theological.

# IV. The Diaconal Family Community as a Way of Building a "Network"

The future lies in the ability to "build a network": the works of God "are all in collaboration. . . . Let's connect. I do not love alone, I love many, with many: I associate myself to live and do charity better."[86] This willingness to "build a network" has within it the seed of family closeness. The family is the prophecy of the Kingdom, it is God's dream, it is the first letter of the alphabet of love. St. Augustine said, "love and you will understand." The relational circularity of the family represents the transition from knowing one another to loving care in line with the principle of love that incorporates all things and that cares for all people. This is even truer for deacons. But the family of deacons is not meant to with-draw into itself in the name of safety or social mistrust, nor should it live removed from its context, its qualita-tive impoverishment as a consequence. On the contrary, the openness of the diaconal family to other families,

---

86    Fr. Primo Mazzolari (1890–1959), Italian writer and pastor who wrote on simplicity and poverty. Pope Francis gave an address on a visit to Fr. Mazzolari's tomb in Italy, June 20, 2017.

to society, and to the parish decreases anxiety about the future, it teaches to share, makes one feel a part of something, and activates new energies. At the diaconal level, the family can help launch new pastoral work that is activated to be "dispersed" throughout the world and that enhances of the vocation of lay Christians in order to be close to the people where they live. The family is the first "minority" that sheds light on society as a whole: "Tell me what kind of family you have and I will tell you what kind of society/future you are building." Rhetorics aside, it is truly necessary to start over from the family, the main social cushion and "village fountain" that continues to provide running water to quench the thirst of modern man. When will we have new politics on the family? When will we have a new diaconal family? Pope Francis is well aware it is not the document's responsibility to provide "a detailed and complete analysis of contemporary reality."[87] Further interpretations and reflections are referred to the communities and pastors. "Clearly"—he says—"Jesus does not want us to be grandees who look down upon others, but men and women of the people. This is not an idea of the Pope, or one pastoral option among others; they are injunctions contained in the word of God."[88] Priests, as well as deacons, are suggested to read the sections on the homily and

---

87   EG, no. 5.
88   EG, no. 271.

preaching (nos. 135-159) to get a sense of the high tension that runs throughout the document: it is not a sense of an apocalyptic or dangerous time, but of a *kairòs*, of a time that is propitious toward the Gospel and favorable to the proclamation of Hope and the regenerative breath of Charity: a service that is proper to deacons.

# V. Deacons, "Do Not Be Afraid of Solidarity!"

Francis has been repeating this exhortation since he was elected—as he likes to say—"Bishop of Rome." In this regard, his rich and courageous Magisterium may effectively be summarized in a sort of "decalogue of solidarity." "Solidarity" is a key word, perhaps one that is overused today, that we as deacons must take on fearlessly so that we can say it with conviction in the Church and in society. This word is not exclusive to Christian vocabulary. On the contrary, it transversely affects the entire human vocabulary, positioning itself as an absolutely indispensable word for the renewal of our societies. *Solidarity* is a fundamentally diaconal word. And it implies something more than a few more or less sporadic acts of generosity: it presumes the creation of a new mindset that is capable of thinking in terms of community and the priority of the life of all over the appropriation of goods by a few.[89] It means restoring to the poor what belongs to them.[90] This meaningful solidarity comes from an attention to the most marginalized, and it asks us to go toward others with empty hands, without prejudice, to understand, accept, and walk with those who are different from us. The first step toward a Church which is poor and for the poor, therefore, is the abandonment of any attempt to build a privileged caste and the awareness of belonging fully to the human family, indeed, wanting to build and safeguard this family through authentic material and spiritual sharing. Leaven in the dough of humanity (cf. Mt 13:33), the Church finds her reason for being when she rejects all vain attempts at separation and gives herself to mending, restoring, and reuniting that which has been divided.

## 1. The right of citizenship to solidarity must be recognized.

Solidarity, while often an unpopular word in the Western economic world, is the treasure of the poor, and the full right of citizenship to it must be recognized. It is not a handout; it is a social value that must be thought of as more than just assistance to the poor, but as a global rethinking of the entire economic system and the pursuit

---

89    Cf. EG, no. 188.

90    Cf. EG, no. 189.

of ways to reform and correct that system in a way that is coherent with the fundamental rights of every man and all men of the earth.

## 2. Solidarity says "no" to the culture of waste.

Solidarity is a word that reflects the human and Christian values that are required of us today to counter the Western culture of waste. It is a culture that always tends to exclude people who are in a state of need or fragility: children, young people, the elderly, all of those who are "useless" because they are no longer in the condition to produce. Now, a people that discards its "weaker sectors," that does not take care of its elderly because they have become a "burden" that is hard to bear, that does not take responsibility for its disabled and their families, that has no concern for its little ones and those "without a voice," a people like that has lost the memory of its humanity and with it, has lost every possibility of a future. We must have the courage to declare: If we do not learn to be more in solidarity, there will be no hope for a future for any country or society.

## 3. Solidarity says "no" to the globalization of indifference.

The culture of prosperity in Western cultures, which is selfishly focused on "me" and on the satisfaction of one's own needs first, makes us insensitive to the cries of others. It closes our relational capacity in soap bubbles that are beautiful, but inconsistent and ephemeral: they offer a fleeting and empty illusion that results in indifference to others. Indeed, it even leads to what we can call, using Pope Francis's words, "the globalization of indifference."[91] Sadly, we have become used to the suffering of others, and therefore, this suffering carries less importance and meaning: it doesn't affect me; it doesn't concern me; it's none of my business! The culture of prosperity that deadens us[92] must, therefore, be contrasted by the culture of generous solidarity[93] that keeps us from being controlled by the logic of productivity and the market and that accepts the ethical laws of respect and promotion of the dignity of each person.

## 4. Solidarity must also be realized through policies inspired by solidarity.

To concretize the value of solidarity, we must "rehabilitate" politics and restore its potential for service to the common good so that it may truly be one of the highest forms of charity. The future demands a humanistic vision of economy and a politics capable of ensuring greater and more effective participation on the part of the people,

---

91   EG, no. 54.

92   Cf. EG, no. 54.

93   Cf. EG, no. 58.

eliminating forms of elitism and eradicating poverty. The primary purpose of politics is to work toward a situation where no one is deprived of what is necessary and where everyone is guaranteed dignity, fraternity, and solidarity. For Christians, working for the common good is a duty, and many times, the way to fulfill this duty is precisely through politics, where tireless effort is made to make the most disadvantaged people the center of attention. The awareness of this difficulty to remove obstacles and discrimination must animate policies that are faithful to man and to the collective. It also makes it clear that citizens, especially Christians, must take an interest in the political reality of their country or territory. At times, this requires making choices that are unpopular but courageous and consistent with the Gospel.

## 5. There is no true peace without solidarity.

It is the task of all men to build peace by two routes: (1) the promotion and practice of justice with truth and love; and (2) everyone contributing, according to his means, to integral human development following the logic of solidarity. This is incontrovertible. But if we look honestly at our social reality, we must ask ourselves to what extent this principle translates into concrete, visible, and credible choices, choices that we could define as "diaconal." There cannot be true peace and harmony if we do not work with conviction and a sense of responsibility for a more just and integral society, and if we do not overcome every level of selfish, individualistic, and group interests.

## 6. Solidarity means serving.

Being in solidarity means "serving," that is, entering into relationships with those who are in need, recognizing them as people, and committing ourselves to finding concrete solutions to their needs, all without calculation or fear and with tenderness and understanding. The deacon is not someone who likes to just talk about the poor. He is someone who meets the poor, looks them in the eyes, touches them. In these people—the hungry, thirsty, naked, sick, and oppressed—he recognizes and finds the wounds of Christ to be healed with solicitude, patience, and tenderness.

## 7. Solidarity means accompanying.

"Accompanying" means not settling for charity that leaves the poor person as he is. True mercy, the mercy God gives to us and teaches us, demands justice. It demands that the poor find the way to be poor no longer. It asks to ensure that no one ever again stand in need of a soup kitchen set up for social emergency, of makeshift lodgings, of a service of legal assistance in order to have his legitimate right recognized to live and to work, to be fully a person.

## 8. Solidarity means defending.

"Defending" means recognizing and accepting requests for justice and hope, and seeking roads together, real paths that lead to liberation. It means taking the side of the weakest. How many times we either don't know how or don't want to give voice to the voice of those who have suffered and who continue to suffer, of those who have seen their own rights trampled upon, of those who have experienced so much violence that it has even stifled the legitimate desire in their hearts to have justice done! Those who are poor, marginalized, and suffering should not be considered "objects of solidarity and charity."[94] They must feel that they are active members in the life and mission of the Church: a place and specific role must be given to them in the parish and in every sector of the Church.

## 9. Solidarity is also knowing how to weep.

Solidarity must bring the Christian to "know how to weep"[95] before tragedies that take place every day to the detriment of the poor. The Christian cannot resign himself to a society that has forgotten the experience

---

94 Pope Francis, Address to the Members of UNITALSI on the Occasion of the 110th Anniversary of Its Foundation (November 9, 2013), no. 2.

95 Pope Francis, Address to Young People at Manila's University of Santo Tomas (January 18, 2015).

of weeping. Sometimes in our lives, tears are precisely the lenses we need to see Jesus. It is not good—as Pope Francis would say—when the Church does not weep.

## 10. *Solidarity means becoming God's caress.*

Every day, Christians are called to become a "caress of God" for those who perhaps have forgotten the intimate joy of their first caresses, or perhaps who have never been able to experience one. Following the example of the Good Samaritan, the Christian does not look the other way in the face of suffering; he always tries to be a welcoming gaze, a helping hand, a word of comfort, a tender embrace.

Following the example of God, who loves to caress us even when we deserve to be reprimanded because God is the Father, each Christian must show mercy toward his brother. The Son of God, by becoming flesh, summoned us to the revolution of tenderness,[96] he who first became the Tenderness of the Father for the world.

# VI. The Diaconia of Pastoral Humility

Pope Francis's pastoral work stands out for its simple language and humble attitudes. At the same time, he asks

---

96   Cf. EG, no. 88.

that the entire Church practice humility in the exercise of her mission. "The style of evangelical preaching—he said—should have this attitude: humility, service, charity, brotherly love. 'But . . . Lord, we must conquer the world!' That word, conquer, doesn't work. We must preach in the world. The Christian must not be like soldiers who when they win the battle make a clean sweep of everything."[97] This is an impassioned reading of the Church's presence in today's world. In the context of today's world, the Church is called to be humble, in imitation of the humility of God himself who, in Jesus Christ, compromised himself with the Earth and humanity, and who allows Her—his Bride—to be a chosen people animated by the Holy Spirit. Consequently, the Church will be humble in listening to the basic questions of the human heart, in proposing—in a credible way—a truth that leads to freedom, and facing the "turnovers of history" to deliver the liberating and healing prophecy of the Gospel. In this context, we can understand the deacon's presence and his being a "prophecy" of Christ the Servant in the community and among the people even more clearly.

Jorge Mario Bergoglio develops his reflection on humility taking inspiration from the Church Father Dorotheus of Gaza (525-634), a fruitful ascetic writer and one of the most widely read of the Byzantine monastic

---

97  Pope Francis, Homily (April 25, 2013).

tradition. For Dorotheus, the Christian's great struggle does not lie in outer asceticism but in the asceticism of the ego, in the discipline of the ego, or rather in the sacrificing "one's own will" to seek the common good and to consent to the will of God: "How can anyone bear another person or listen to advice when he is attached to his own will?" He focuses first on the temptations that the ego is exposed to. The first temptation is the "temptation to individualism," which—Bergoglio reminds us—is the proud attitude of the religious person when he lives to make everything about him. This temptation often puts the lives of deacons at risk as well by convincing them, at times, of the *factiousness of community life* or to withdraw into an individualism of convenience that proliferates, rather than overcomes, the underlying roots of "suspicion and distrust." Now, if humility is the virtuous force that pushes us to encounter our brother and to take communion with him, then "the spirit of suspicion and distrust . . . essentially leads to a truth that protects me against my brother." In a speech to deacons at a meeting of catechists, Cardinal Bergoglio said, "Be deacons, that is to say, servants who are almost obsessed with communion. Let yourselves be involved by the Spirit, who invites us to overcome our individualism and our feeling like we are not involved. Let's let go of the mentality of the old and nostalgic adage 'nothing is going right' that causes us to run after the prophets of misfortune to find ourselves already old and tired. There is too much pain in the world today. And there are many sad faces, even among those who believe in the Good News of the Gospel, and they hide the joy of Easter. It is for them that we must proclaim with joy that Jesus is the Lord; it is a deep joy that comes from the Lord's presence throughout our history."[98] It is a divisive spirit because—as Bergoglio writes, recalling Ignatius of Loyola—"it is the Devil himself who plants suspicion in the hearts in order to divide." The ascetic trace of Dorotheus and the piercing words of Bergoglio bring the ascetic eye to descend upon the recesses of the spirit where Christian spiritual life, though imbued with evangelical simplicity, also possesses a great skill that requires spiritual guidance—which must always be the backdrop of our diaconal actions—and common sense, which is always necessary for our service. Diaconal spirituality, therefore, is a source of strength against global challenges.

# VII. The Deacon as a Disciple and Pastor

When studying Bergoglio's writings, one thing that jumps out at the eye, and even more so to one's sense of being a believer, is that he is pursuing a "discipular" Church model, even if the actual concept and word almost

---

98    Speech Given at the Opening of the Meeting of Catechists, Buenos Aires (March 12, 2005).

never appear. We could say that the *discipularitas* is seen throughout his writings and his words on the Church. This is especially evident in his attempt to deconstruct a "self-referential Church" that presents itself—as we know—as a self-sought, self-realized, and self-motivated reality. Bergoglio cultivates an idea of a *discipular Church* that rejects any form of Church so imbued with a "worldliness" that it forgets its rise *ex alto* and its "fontal" being in close relationship with Christ. For this reason, his speech on the Church starts with Christ (this is the discipular movement): he thinks of the Church as a reality of grace that Christ *founds, forms, and reforms*. Let's take a closer look at these three dimensions.

## Jesus Founds the Church

Bergoglio talks about a Church founded in Christ in the spiritual exercises preached to the bishops of Spain (2006). He connects the singular "foundation" of the Church to when Christ gives the mission to pastors. He writes: "When the Lord gives us our mission, he founds our being. He does not do so in a merely functional way, like one who gives someone a job or occupation. Rather he does it with the power of his Spirit, in such a way that we belong to the mission and our very identity is indelibly marked by it. . . . Jesus founds us in his Church . . . The basic foundational attitude is to let oneself be formed in the Church. Jesus wants men who are rooted and founded in the Church."[99] Bergoglio also specifies the "foundation" of the Church in a pastoral way, connecting it to the topic of formation: Christ founds the Church by founding hearts. He talks about letting the Lord "found us anew" and "as pastors," and about the commitment to found Christian hearts inherent in the mandate. It is an idea of strong theological fiber and rare spiritual elegance, but also of unsettling existential truth. Thus, he affirms: "In the exercise of our ministry [diaconal], we are thus collaborating with Christ to found . . . Christian hearts . . . at the same time as we go about this very same work, the Lord founds and roots our heart in his."

## Jesus Forms the Church, Making Her His Bride

The idea of the Church being "founded" by Jesus also affects the form he gives her. She is a Bride and Mother, modeled after Mary: "Jesus founds the Church, and he found us in the Church. The mystery of the Church is intimately bound to the mystery of Mary, the mother of God and the Mother of the Church. Mary gives birth to us and takes care of us. So does the Church. . . . This is the Church our faithful people revere. Therefore, when

---

99 Cardinal Jorge Mario Bergoglio, *In Him Alone Is Our Hope: The Church According to the Heart of Pope Francis* (New York: Magnificat, 2013).

we speak about the Church, we need to feel the same devotion as we do for the Virgin Mary." Adapting the thought of Isaac of Stella which states: *Maria et Ecclesia, una mater et plures* (Mary and the Church are one mother, yet more than one mother), Bergoglio states that Mary and the Church are only one bride, only one mother. He returns to the topic of the Church as Bride in talking about the Epiphany: "The three mysteries are united in the vision of a wedding feast: the bridegroom is Christ the Messiah, who loves the Church as his bride and sacrificed himself for her (cf. Eph 5:25), purifying her in the baptismal waters and making her His. And there is talk of a wedding . . . a wedding party where the guests participate and bring gifts." Mary, therefore, is a "model, an icon for diaconal activity." Mary is a luminous model of diaconal ministry. Guided by the Spirit, she declared herself a servant (*diàkonos*) of the Lord with such simplicity in the exact moment that, by power of the Holy Spirit, she was to become the Mother of Christ.

## Jesus Reforms the Church

Jesus is the permanent, and only, Master and deacon of the Church. It is his task to teach even by means of correcting or reprimanding because, in him, correction and reprimand are perfectly reconciled with loving and saving grace. Bergoglio writes: "From the Lord's hand comes his abundant mercy." His role as educator is also exercised toward pastors of the Church. The Lord reprimands our "expulsive tendency," that is, the tendency of pastors (and sometimes deacons) to "exclude" people—rather than include them—from the community or the discipleship, an attitude that is caused by a lack of charity. Priests are reminded of what the People of God ask of them, one request being that "they are in deep communion with the bishop, the other priests, and the deacons."[100] Jesus reprimands us for the fears that arise from our lack of faith: "Out of fear of being unable to lead the flock"—he exemplifies—"[we sometimes] try to rise above the difficult situation." The Lord reprimands us for our weaknesses that come from our lack of hope. "One does not invent the cross, nor does one take it up as if it were an unavoidable fate; this is why, when we do not carry the cross of our mission, even as deacons, we no longer taste hope." Lastly—the future pope wrote—the Lord reprimands the pastor for his inability to keep watch with him. In a powerful final observation, he warns: "What I wish to underline here is the particular depth in what it means to keep watch, compared with supervision in the broader sense or watchful vigilance in a stricter sense. . . . To be vigilant it is enough to be awake, alert, and shrewd. To keep watch requires meekness, patience, and the constancy of tested charity." One who dedicates himself to "being vigilant" (and alert, as

---

100 *Aparecida* Message to Priests, Brochero (September 11, 2008).

Bergoglio says) is more of a soldier than a pastor. Only he who keeps watch with a flexible mind and an open heart is fully a pastor, and the Church that he "keeps watch over" is a family, where he lives and serves willingly. It is interesting to look at this quote, even if it is long, from an audience held last March[101] in which Francis talks about the Sacrament of Holy Orders "in its three grades of bishop, priest and deacon." Here, he states that "it is the Sacrament that enables a man to exercise the ministry which the Lord Jesus entrusted to the Apostles, to shepherd his flock, in the power of his Spirit and according to his Heart. Tending Jesus' flock not by the power of human strength or by one's own power, but by the Spirit's and according to his Heart, the Heart of Jesus which is a heart of love." It is interesting to note the emphasis given to the oneness of the sacrament where it reads that it is the responsibility of "the priest, the bishop, the deacon [to] shepherd the Lord's flock with love. It is useless if it is not done with love" (here it is assumed that the subject remains "the bishop, the priest, and the deacon"). "And in this sense, the ministers"— meaning all three—"who are chosen and consecrated for this service extend Jesus' presence in time, if they do so by the power of the Holy Spirit, in God's name and with love." Here, the pope continues to talk about three aspects of the ordained ministry as a whole, although, to

---

101  Pope Francis, General Audience (March 26, 2014).

tell the truth, the diaconate seems to get lost along the way. This is how he explains the three aspects:

1.    A first aspect. Those who are ordained are placed *at the head of the community*. They are "at the head," yes, but for Jesus this means placing one's authority *at the service* [of the community], as Jesus himself showed and taught his disciples with these words: "You know that the rulers of the Gentiles lord it over them, and their great men exercise authority over them. It shall not be so among you; but whoever would be great among you must be your servant, and whoever would be first among you must be your slave; even as the Son of man came not to be served but to serve, and to give his life as a ransom for many" (Mt 20:25-28; Mk 10:42-45). A bishop who is not at the service of the community fails to perform his duty; a priest who is not at the service of his community fails to perform his duty, he errs.

2.    Another characteristic which also derives from this sacramental union with Christ is *a passionate love for the Church*. . . . Through Holy Orders the minister dedicates himself entirely to his community and loves it with all his heart: it is his family. . . . How? As Christ loves the Church. St. Paul will say the same of marriage: the husband

is to love his wife as Christ loves the Church. It is a great mystery of love: this of priestly ministry and that of matrimony are two Sacraments, pathways which people normally take to go to the Lord.

3. A final aspect. The Apostle Paul recommends to the disciple Timothy that he not neglect, indeed, that *he always rekindle the gift that is within him*. The gift that he has been given through the laying on of hands (cf. 1 Tm 4:14; 2 Tm 1:6).

# VIII. The Diaconia of Mercy

"Be merciful, even as your Father is merciful" (Lk 6:36). This teaching that the Lord gave to his disciples in the Gospel and that St. Luke set down is the message Pope Francis has been echoing since the beginning of his papacy. We owe it to him and his exhortation *Evangelii Gaudium* for having brought about what we can define as a return to the focal point of Christian life. In fact, is proper to every renewal of the Church or spiritual return to the source to bring about this "re-aligning" with the Gospel, from which the burdens of everyday life never cease to distract us. The heart of God's message is mercy. By underlining this shocking reality, which invests and transfigures every aspect of the human experience with newness, the pope throws open the doors of newfound consolation to all and encourages every Christian to put Christ back at the center of one's heart despite one's personal limits and with the absolute certainty that one can count on the merciful acceptance of His grace. "Jesus"—the pope says—"speaks only a word of forgiveness, not of condemnation," and his promise to the good thief, he adds, "gives us great hope: it tells us that God's grace is always greater than the prayer which sought it."[102] So, when God finds himself before those who are considered evil, the sinners, those "with no hope of conversion," not only does he not threaten, punish, or castigate them, but he envelops them in love and tenderness. Pope Francis's exhortation insistently reminds us of this disconcerting news: *God never tires of forgiving us; we are the ones who tire of seeking his mercy* (EG, no. 3). Francis calls us to go beyond the closed fences on our journey, the journey toward salvation, to go beyond our ways of thinking that are ingrained with our judgment to go toward the inclusive and trusting acceptance of the other, and to transcend time toward eternity on the path of humanity, which is, at the same time, the path of Christ and of the Church. So, what is mercy? Quoting St. Thomas Aquinas, Pope Francis defines it like this: "In itself mercy is the greatest of the virtues, since all the others revolve around it and, more than this, it makes up for their deficiencies. This is particular

---

102 Pope Francis, Homily at Mass for the Conclusion of the Year of Faith (November 24, 2013).

to the superior virtue, and as such it is proper to God to have mercy, through which his omnipotence is manifested to the greatest degree."[103] Mercy, therefore, is the form Love takes to free man from sin and keep him away from evil when "on the cross . . . Jesus endured in his own flesh the dramatic encounter of the sin of the world and God's mercy."[104] In the radical divine gift that is the sending of his Son and his Death on the Cross, we find the most obvious demonstration that God's forgiveness precedes man's repentance. Mercy, therefore, does not merely indicate a feeling, nor does it conclude with a more or less sporadic gesture of human availability, but, in a much more meaningful and concrete way, it is an *activity*, an intentional and effective action that allows us to recognize a *person* who constantly wishes to establish a regenerative and joyful encounter with us. "Blessed are the merciful," according to Pope Francis, does not mean carving out a specific moment for kindness toward others; it means creating an existential *habitus*, because it is only when we *habitually* do good and *habitually* help others that we too can find mercy. God identifies with the oppressed, with history's victims, and shares in the suffering of the poor and needy. The pope writes, "The apostle James teaches that our mercy to others will vindicate us on the day of God's judgment. . . . Mercy triumphs

103 EG, no. 37.
104 EG, no. 285.

over judgment (2:12-13). Here James is faithful to the finest tradition of post-exilic Jewish spirituality, which attributed a particular salutary value to mercy."[105] This shows the urgency to assume Christian behavior that is rooted in the Beatitudes and that, through the behavior of Christ's disciples, restores the face of Christ himself, Christ who is meek and humble of heart. The true face of God, face that is gift and forgiveness, is at play. Also at play, consequently, is the true face of man.

# Conclusion

As deacons who are called to "journey, build and confess" (words addressed to cardinals at the beginning of his papacy), today we can restore ourselves and regain our strength to show our world once again the face of the simple and authentic things. The Bishop of Rome has presented the diaconal ministry with a great challenge and it must not be ignored. The gesture he made at the beginning of his papacy by washing feet—as he used to do in Buenos Aires—while wearing the diaconal stole is a very powerful sign that places the poor and marginalized at the center; it is a sign of evangelical *parrhesia* for the world. For a long time, theologians, bishops, and even deacons themselves have been in search of the identity of the diaconate. Even though his teachings

---

105 EG, no. 193.

do not explicitly refer to the diaconal ministry, Francis presents the community with a clear vision of a diaconal Church. This vision incorporates the best of scholarly work, theological reflection, and historical research. It considers service to the poor and the suffering and prophetic opposition to injustice to be acts of Christian charity. But it also includes reaching those who are poor spiritually, those who seek the truth, those who are far from God, those who have never been Christians, and those who no longer believe. The pope sent a hand-written letter[106] on the occasion of the Ordination of deacons in Buenos Aires in which he emphasized that the existence and exercise of the diaconal ministry must be characterized by service, as this ministry is the public expression and manifestation of the vocation to service itself . . . and this is not only for a limited time but for a lifetime, permanently: "Service for Jesus Christ, service for the Church, and service to brothers, especially the poorest and those most in need. Don't be 'part-time deacons' or functionaries. The Church is not an NGO. May service enhance your lives. Like deacon Lawrence—put flesh to fire."

The Synod on the New Evangelization can help us properly contextualize deacons in the New Evangelization. In the *Lineamenta*, the following question

---

106 Letter addressed to Msgr. Joaquín Sucunza to be read at the end of the celebration of the Ordination of deacons in the Buenos Aires Cathedral.

is formulated: "How has the ministry of the permanent diaconate been included in the Church's mandate to evangelize?"[107] Later, in the "proposition" on the pastoral dimension of the diaconal ministry, the document recognizes and encourages the work of deacons, whose ministry renders a great service to the Church. Programs of ongoing formation for deacons in the dioceses are also called for.[108] Gospel proclamation in the particular Church, which is the subject of the New Evangelization, requires the collaboration of priests, deacons, and consecrated and lay people. This is so because in each place, the particular Church is the concrete manifestation of the Church of Christ and as such initiates, coordinates, and accomplishes the pastoral actions through which the New Evangelization is carried out.[109]

In the Apostolic Exhortation *Evangelii Gaudium*, Pope Francis encourages priests and deacons to find new paths and tools suitable for today's world in order

---

107 Synod of Bishops, XIII Ordinary General Assembly, *The New Evangelization for the Transmission of the Christian Faith*, Lineamenta 22, "Evangelizers and Educators as Witnesses," no. 30.

108 Proposition 49, "Pastoral Dimension of the Ordained Ministry."

109 Proposition 41, "New Evangelization and the Particular Church."

to make preaching more relevant and "appealing."[110]
Scripture shows us a man who is a perfect example of
this profile of the diaconate: it is Philip, one of the seven
who were chosen to help the Apostles (Acts 6:1-10).
Acts 21:8 even calls Philip an "evangelist." He combines the service of the tables—the ministry to widows
and the poor—with the courageous work of proclaiming
Christ in times of persecution (Acts 8:4-8). While he
was bringing the Good News, he encountered Simon
the magician (Acts 8:9-25) and lead the Ethiopian officer to Christ after explaining the Scripture to him (Acts
8:26-39). He then continued his ministry while systematically trying to evangelize the towns along the coast of
the Mediterranean as far as Caesarea (Acts 8:40). Philip,
a deacon and evangelist, is the biblical figure who best
represents the vision of a diaconate that is called to proclaim the Gospel. While this wonderful description of
the diaconal ministry testifies to the growing approval
that the diaconate has met over time, it also helps us
understand that deacons are, in reality, *signs* for the

---

110 Cf. EG, III, "Preparing to preach": "Another feature of a good homily
is that it is positive. It is not so much concerned with pointing out
what shouldn't be done, but with suggesting what we can do better. In
any case, if it does draw attention to something negative, it will also
attempt to point to a positive and attractive value, lest it remain mired
in complaints, laments, criticisms and reproaches. Positive preaching
always offers hope, points to the future, does not leave us trapped in
negativity. How good it is when priests, deacons and the laity gather
periodically to discover resources which can make preaching more
attractive!" (no. 159).

Church of all that it should do. It would be misleading, in fact, to describe and evaluate the diaconate solely in terms of its function. This requires a "new incarnation" of diaconia in the most troubled places of our time. It requires careful listening to the "cry of the poor" in the most diverse situations of our existence, situations that often cannot be immediately assimilated to the common experience because they derive from unresolved conflicts, ethnic prejudices, and socioeconomic and political conditions that have given way to new kinds of poverty, new questions of meaning, and new challenges for our capacity for dialogue and change. The ecumenical exchange of ideas and experiences is a fundamental place for different forms of ministerial diaconia to meet, understand, and enrich one another in order to proclaim the Gospel of hope and peace to all men: a proclamation that can become concrete and liberating "service" anywhere and for anyone. Now especially, in light of Pope Francis's Magisterium, the diaconal ministry must be understood as and considered an integral part of the work carried out by the Council to prepare the entire Church for a renewed apostolate in today's world, in a world that thirsts for renewal, answers, hope, and peace, a world in which deacons are called to reach out to their brothers and share their anxieties and hopes in tireless, faithful, and luminous service that makes them "pioneers of the new civilization of love."[111]

The following pages will examine the words spoken by Pope Francis as Cardinal Bergoglio in the Diocese of Buenos Aires and now as pope.

The texts will be introduced by brief theological reflections to help us take stock, although not completely, of Francis's thought and of how he understands the diaconal ministry.

The following reflections, therefore, are merely a modest contribution that requires further study. They combine theological reflection, which is always necessary, and the experience and Magisterium of the pope.

---

111  Pope John Paul II, General Audience (February 8, 1995).

# Cardinal Jorge Mario Bergoglio, SJ

# PART IV
# The Diaconal Ecclesiology of Communion

Before becoming pope, Cardinal Bergoglio ventured an interpretation of conciliar documents for the purpose of preparing a pastoral renewal of the catechesis in the Buenos Aires diocese, especially as regards communion.

He invited deacons to overcome every form of individualism in order to be "servants who are obsessed with communion."

Today, *communion* is increasingly at the center of the Church's reflection and serves as a hermeneutic lens to understand the complex ecclesiology of Vatican II. Paraphrasing *Lumen Gentium*, paragraph 1, the Church is a *sacrament of communion with God, and communion among people*. The Church is a sign of communion and it generates communion both with God and among the people.

Our parish communities are often no longer able to take on the global nature of the Church's mission or to give life to a community and authentic communion for an evangelizing and charitable presence. This observation should urge us to structure the life and apostolic commitment of communities in a community in which Gospel proclamation, dialogue of faith, common prayer, and service to brothers can take on a more human dimension. This conversion of mentality and style requires qualified animators and persons in charge who, in communion with the bishop and priests, take responsibility for a service that has become indispensable and delicate. On the other hand, the need is always growing in our local Churches for a pastoral ministry that goes to where people live to proclaim the Gospel of charity and to give them a deeper ecclesial experience. Even in these places, the presence of a deacon who has been chosen and sent by the bishop can serve as a valuable link between the person with full and ultimate responsibility and the people.

The reestablishment of the diaconate is, in a way, a kind of testing ground for the collective soul-searching that was Vatican II. The identity and ministry of the deacon, in fact, refer to the four conciliar constitutions: the Church as a mystery and sacrament (*Lumen Gentium*), the priority of listening to and proclaiming the Word of God (*Dei Verbum*), the primacy of liturgy, the summit and source of the life of the Church (*Sacrosanctum Concilium*), the relationship between this and the world and the urgency of a New Evangelization in the current situation (*Gaudium et Spes*). Reflection on the diaconate and on the reception in our Churches of the conciliar decisions relative to it allow us to broaden the horizon to the entire life and mission of the Church in our time. Strictly speaking, what the Council reestablished was *"the principle of the permanent exercise of the diaconate,* and not one particular form which the diaconate had taken in the past."[112]

In other words, the Second Vatican Council seemed open to the form this ministry could have taken in the future depending on pastoral needs and Church practice, while remaining faithful to tradition. One of the predominant features of the Council was that, in a way, it tempered the more cerebral, intellectual, and scholastic approach to the Catholic faith of the second millennium, making a healthy return to the wisdom of the Fathers of the first millennium, especially of the first centuries. For this reason, every possible reflection on the diaconate and every correct understanding of its diversified and flexible journey throughout the centuries has to trace back to the diaconia of the ordained ministry found in the mentality inaugurated by the Council, or better yet, in the *heart* of conciliar ecclesiology, that is, the *ecclesiology of communion* that inspired the Magisterium in the years following Vatican II and has marked the rhythm the Church's life ever since. The journey initiated by the conciliar assembly found further development and explanation in post-conciliar Magisterium, resulting in a broader outlook on the ecumenical context, where the

---

112 International Theological Commission, *From the Diakonia of Christ to the Diakonia of the Apostles* (Vatican City: LEV, 2003).

diaconate is already a living presence and a multifarious "promise" of dialogue, hope, and peace.

The unifying principle and hermeneutic key to all conciliar Magisterium is *the ecclesiology of communion*.

The first thing it calls for is a maturation within communities of what the documents call the "diaconal conscience," or rather the awareness of "communionality" that translates into participation and shared responsibility at all levels and in its many forms.

Another point of reference, which is closely tied to the first, concerns the central role acquired by local and particular Churches in the exercise of ministries, as they are the manifestation or occurrence of the *catholica*, that is, the universal Church. First of all, the deacon's relationship with the bishop must be one of communion and must be permeated with obedience. This relationship must also extend to all other members of the Church and to the pastoral project of the diocese. In this perspective, it also understood that the diaconal ministry does not belong to the parish itself; this is also to keep the deacon from being considered a kind of "assistant priest."

One visible and concrete manifestation of the Church as communion is the annual Chrism Mass. Church is understood there not as a privilege nor a power but a challenge and a task. It is a challenge to be a sacrament of communion in our too-fragmented and divided world, a world that lacks wholeness and health. Vatican II said that the Liturgy, especially the Eucharist, is the highest manifestation of the Church's true nature. This is most evident in the Chrism Mass. The Chrism Mass is at the heart of this challenge of the Church to be a living sacrament of communion for two reasons. First, in the ordinary course of the liturgical year, the Chrism Mass is the only occasion in which the local Church is most fully represented. At its center is the bishop. "The bishop, as such, is a 'sacrament,' i.e., a visible and effacious sign of Christ the 'High Priest,' . . . Through [the bishop], the Christian people in the diocese have every sacrament: he consecrates the holy chrism, he ordains priests, every Eucharist is celebrated in communion with him. . . . Here is what is mirrored in the Chrism Mass: the bishop, priests, deacons, and the faithful of a local Church are gathered for the blessing of the holy oils."[113]

The Chrism Mass is a powerful sacramental expression of the entire gathered Church, the sacrament of communion with God and of communion among all the peoples of the earth. The Collect reads:

Father,
by the power of the Holy Spirit
you anointed your only Son Messiah and Lord of
    creation;

---

113 "Holy Thursday: The Last Supper," *Days of the Lord: The Liturgical Year*, Vol. 3, Easter Triduum/Easter Season, trans. Greg LaNave and Donald Molloy (Collegeville, MN: Liturgical Press/OSB, 1993) 9-10. Originally published in French as *Jours de Seigneur* (Brepols: Publications de Saint-André, 1988).

you have given us share in his consecration
to priestly service in your Church.
Help us to be faithful witnesses in the world
to the salvation Christ won for all humankind.[114]

This prayer implies that each and every one of us through Baptism and Confirmation is given to share in the consecration of Christ to the priestly service, that we are called to be Christ the Priest. In the Preface we find the words:

Christ . . . adorns with a royal priesthood
the people he has made his own[115]

There is no room for individualism here, but rather a mighty sense of being made one priestly people in Christ through God's sacramental action in the Church. The priesthood of all the faithful and the ministerial priesthood share in the one priesthood of Christ, but differently. The whole tenor of the celebration of the Chrism Mass tends is to underscore our joint consecration to be a communion of witness and service in and to our world.

The second reason is this: in the Chrism Mass, we renew our vows—priests, deacons, religious, and laity—even if in common practice it is only priests who actually

114 Opening Prayer for the Chrism Mass, *The Roman Missal: Sacramentary* (New York: Catholic Book Publishing Co., 1985) 131.

115 Preface for the Chrism Mass, *Roman Missal, Third Edition* (Washington, DC: USCCB, 2011) 1140.

renew their vows. *We show God to the world* by making our vows—baptismal, ministerial—and by keeping them. The fidelity, the day-to-day keeping of the vow, points to and sacramentalizes God's fidelity to his creation, and especially to us. It is one thing to say that one will give everything, offer all that one is now, and it is another to promise to go on year after year, no matter what happens. God remains utterly faithful to us. The vows taken in Baptism, in Ordination, in religious life participate in that divine faithfulness and render visible to others the loving faithfulness that God is. The Chrism Mass is an ecclesial statement of the Church's identity as communion, and a public statement and pledge to the world that our lives will be a visible portrayal of the infinite love God is and has for every human. In an age that finds commitment until death extraordinarily difficult, the commitments in the Chrism Mass could not be more significant.

The oil of Chrism invites Catholics to reaffirm as deeply and personally as possible our configuration to Christ through Baptism, Confirmation, and Ordination. The oil of the sick invites Catholics to recognize our identity in illness and to conjoin our sufferings to the One in whom we live and move and have our being. The oil of catechumens is intended to strengthen those among us who are making their way into the Church, those who are preparing for incorporation, for embodiment in Christ. Thus, priests, deacons, religious, and all the faithful, including the sick and the elect—baptized and confirmed and ordained and about to be baptized and confirmed—are called to be this "chrismed" presence of Christ in the world.

As Church, we are not only the manifestation or showing forth of communion with God but also an effective help in God's hands: the reality that, evangelized by God, evangelizes for God, and reconciled with God, reconciles with God, and drawn together by God, draws together for God. The Chrism Mass gives us this primal sense and concrete expression of the Church as communion. All are called to *service in communion* as Church. Christians serve each other by loving each other! In fraternal *koinonìa*, one learns and exercises Christian *diakonìa. The service of charity*, therefore, holds first place in the Church. It is a service that ordained ministers should first offer to one another.

For this reason, we are strongly urged to live our Christian vocation with "humility and gentleness, with patience" (Eph 4:2). At the same time, we are invited to use our ministerial perfection to "serve one another through love" (Gal 5:13); that is, we are called to support one another in service, "to bear one another's burdens, and . . . fulfill the law of Christ" (Gal 6:2), his "new commandment" (Jn 13:34) of gratuitous and mutual willing love, "as" he willingly loved us. This is the Church!

This is the Church that Pope Francis wants!

# The Words of Cardinal Bergoglio

## Speech Given at the Beginning of the Archdiocesan Meeting of Catechists

*He went up the mountain and summoned*
*those whom he wanted and they came to him.*
*He appointed twelve [whom he also named*
*apostles] that they might be with him and he*
*might send them forth to preach.*

Mk 3:13-14

Each year, catechists gather in the EAC (*Encuentro Arquidiocesano de Catequesis*), which is synonymous with communion. For one day, they leave their work in the parish to experience the richness of communion, the marvelous symphony of diversities and similarities. It is a day of sharing, reciprocal enrichment, and common experience in the courtyard of La Salle, and it is a day for the many people who, week after week, proclaim Jesus to those large and small. They live this experience in spiritual communion with all of the other members of the community of the faithful and pastoral workers. These days of grace will be a contribution and commitment for the entire diocesan assembly. Be deacons, that is to say, servants who are almost obsessed with communion. Let yourselves be involved by the Spirit, who invites us to overcome our individualism and our feeling like we are not involved. Let's let go of the mentality of the old and nostalgic adage "nothing is going right" that causes us to run after the prophets of misfortune to find ourselves already old and tired. There is too much pain in the world today. And there are many sad faces, even among those who believe in the Good News of the Gospel, and they hide the joy of Easter. It is for them that we must proclaim with joy that Jesus is the Lord; it is a deep joy that comes from the Lord's presence throughout our history.

Buenos Aires, March 12, 2005

# Speech at the First Meeting of the Priest's Council

Mission becomes the paradigm of all evangelization. Personal conversion arouses the ability to submit everything to the service of the establishment of the Kingdom of life. Bishops, priests, permanent deacons, consecrated persons, lay persons, are all called to take up an attitude of permanent pastoral conversion, which implies listening with attention and discernment to "what the Spirit says to the churches" (Rev 2:29) through the signs of the times where God manifests himself. May we be fascinated, attracted, seized by the love of Christ so we may say with St. Paul, "Woe to me if I do not preach it" (1 Cor 9:16). May the Mother of the Lord, who, in particular, knew heaviness of heart, accompany and sustain us in our daily trials, and may she obtain for us the grace of evangelical boldness, zeal, and constancy of apostolic mission.

Buenos Aires, April 15, 2008

# PART V

# The Diaconate and Widespread Pastoral Presence

Bergoglio presents a particularly interesting reflection for the understanding of the diaconal ministry and its pastoral activity, namely, the possibility for deacons to keep basic communities. The document *La Restaurazione del Diaconato Permanente in Italia* (*Restoration of the Permanent Diaconate in Italy*) from December 1971 is interesting for the fundamental role it played in the reintroduction of the diaconate into the Italian Church. In this document, the diaconate is seen as the gift of "sacramental grace" destined to "deepen ecclesial communion," to "revive the commitment to mission," to promote "the sense of community and of family spirit of the people of God," and to "accentuate the community and missionary dimensions of the Church and pastoral work" with the aim of "more widespread evangelization" for the "salvation of humanity."[116] The deacon must promote "widespread pastoral presence"[117] and become the

---

116 Italian Episcopal Conference, *La Restaurazione del Diaconato Permanente in Italia* (December 8, 1971), cf. art. 6, 8, 9, 16.

117 *Restaurazione*, art 16.

leader of "lesser communities," which are seen as articulations of parishes.[118]

Therefore, the service of the deacon can make a valuable contribution within the context of pastoral care characterized by the concreteness of immediate interpersonal relationships that allows for the "sharing" of every joy and every pain. This is precisely why, in the document *Norme e Directive* (*Norms and Directives*), the Italian bishops state that "smaller communities, where the authenticity of human relationships facilitates the exercise of charity and service, are more conducive to the diaconal ministry." The Italian bishops wish for the transformation of our parish communities so that "by organizing into lesser communities, they might acquire deeper community physiognomy and therefore greater effectiveness in the widespread evangelization aimed at all of humanity."[119] Thus, the deacon, like his characteristic of service, is called to animate ecclesial communities in a networked way. In recent years, this need has only sporadically created a few "cellular" ecclesial communities as intended in Paul VI's document *Evangelii Nuntiandi*, in which it is stated that "they spring from the need to live the Church's life more intensely, or from the desire and quest for a more human dimension such

---

118 *Restaurazione*, art. 19.

119 Italian Episcopal Conference, *Norme e Direttive, per l'applicazione del documento la Restaurazione del diaconato permanente nella Chiesa italiana* (1972).

as larger ecclesial communities can only offer with difficulty," coming together "for the purpose of listening to and meditating on the Word, for the sacraments and the bond of the agape, groups of people who are linked by age, culture, civil state or social situation: married couples, young people, professional people, etc.; people who already happen to be united in the struggle for justice, brotherly aid to the poor, human advancement."[120] This organization of parish communities would allow for more immediate relationships, the communion of life, and the witness of charity, allowing deacons to promote the right services for the concrete needs in the parish community. So, like the People of God, deacons live and fulfill their mission according to the concrete historical context in which their ministry is carried out.

This kind of pastoral approach also means, as Pope Benedict XVI says, "promot[ing] a renewed season of evangelization"[121] in neighborhoods, residential areas, families, and the areas farthest from the parish. This will lead to the gradual organizational transformation of the community in which the different components of the People of God become more valuable. The creation of interfamily groups that are guided and animated by deacons, especially by reading and referencing the Word of God, will bring out the different aspects of ecclesial

---

120 EN, no. 58.

121 Pope Benedict XVI, Address to Bishops Gathered for the 61st General Assembly of the Italian Episcopal Conference (May 27, 2010).

vocation (communion, service, and witness) that will then have to come together in parish pastoral councils, which are instruments of harmonization and evangelical co-responsibility.

This prospective, which sees deacons working alongside priests, allows for different options for service:

- The deacon as a promoter of the charity directed toward the poorest, whether that means economic, moral, or spiritual poverty. This orientation implies sharing and a preferential option for the poorest that must translate into the option for "effective poverty." "The preferential option and making oneself poor mean not only electing the poor as the privileged subjects of salvation, but also looking at God, the world, and history from their point of view. A God who orders handouts and help for the poor is liked, but a God who asks us to put ourselves in their condition is troublesome and causes scandal."[122]

  This preference must translate into a search for those with the most urgent needs. Thus, it is the task of the entire Christian community to know how to read the *signs of the times* in the perspective of the great horizon of hope in the Book of Revelation—"I make all things new" (Rev

---

122 Cf. Caritas Italiana, *Lo Riconobbero nello Spezzare il Pane*, Pastoral Card (April 16, 1995), no. 5.

21:5); especially for the sick whose suffering is conquered by love.[123] Love requires concreteness above all else.

- The deacon as an animator of the liturgy and particularly of domestic celebrations of the Word. He must exercise this service in a way that reminds people that every expression of Christian life finds "its source and summit" in the Liturgy.

- The deacon as an animator of educational work in its various parts (children, young people, adults) or occasions (celebration of sacraments). "It is a matter of creating meaningful experiences which require support and coordination. In these experiences, the faithful of all ages and conditions can experience the richness of authentic fraternal relationships, be formed to listen to the Word and to exercise communal discernment, and gain the capacity to effectively witness the Gospel in society."[124]

The presence of immediate personal relationships creates the most favorable conditions for giving attention to the needs of people and groups and so, for making

---

123 Cf. Pope John Paul II, *Salvifici Doloris*, Apostolic Letter on the Christian Meaning of Human Suffering (February 11, 1984), no. 14

124 Cf. Italian Episcopal Conference, *Educare alla vita buona del Vangelo*, no. 43.

space for the co-responsibility of the faithful in the exercise of different services and ministries, in accordance with their charisms. The Italian Episcopate has been expressing this need since the beginning of the restoration of the permanent diaconate in the Italian Church. The bishops find it "important that parishes, by organizing into lesser communities, acquire deeper community physiognomy and therefore greater effectiveness in the widespread evangelization aimed at all of humanity."[125]

This document also states that "even in the Italian Church, the need is felt for community promotion of the people of God and for more widespread evangelization through widespread pastoral presence,"[126] and "there are many examples of parishes that have been divided into lesser communities in which zealous men already exercise a ministry of animation with a spirit of service, so it seems appropriate that the diaconal ordination confer upon them the corresponding sacramental grace."[127]

These directives find confirmation when the bishops state that "the diaconate helps form the Church and give it a more complete image that better corresponds to Christ's design and that is more capable, through inner spiritual strength, of adapting to a society that is in need of evangelical and charitable fermentation in

---

125 Cf. *Norme e Direttive*.

126 *Norme e Direttive*, no. 16.

127 *Norme e Direttive*, no. 19.

small groups, neighborhoods, and residential areas. The experiences that some dioceses have had so far are very promising and are being developed."[128]

In this context, the organization of parishes into basic ecclesial communities can facilitate the creation of territorial areas of influence called *deaconries*.

Understanding how deaconries have emerged throughout the history of the Church can help us understand how they can be promoted and developed, even today, as an important reality and opportunity for the diaconal ministry.

Let's look at fifth-century Rome. The city was divided into seven ecclesiastical regions entrusted to the same number of deacons. This was done to better organize the collection of *voluntariae oblationes*: in Roman places of worship, during celebrations, the faithful gave their offerings to the *regionary* deacons who then, during the pontifical Liturgy in the Lateran, placed them on one of the seven altars near the papal altar. This practice is also confirmed by the celebration of the *festa delle collette* (lit., Feast of the Collections), which dates back to apostolic times. According to the indications of Pope Leo the Great (440-461), the collection, which usually took place July 5-15 but could be repeated during Lent or the Ember Days, was not to take place in only one place or one Church, but *omnes regionum vestrarum ecclesias*.

---

128 *Norme e Direttive*, no. 60.

Based on historical, archaeological,[129] and urbanistic criteria, the Roman deaconries were reaffirmed under Gregory the Great (595-604) in order to integrate and decentralize the charitable activities of the Lateran, which was too far away from the most densely populated area of the city. Archaeological data leads us to think that the following deaconries were present in the city at that time: Santa Maria in Cosmedin, San Giorgio in Velabro, San Teodoro, and Santa Maria in Via Lata.

Hence, we must develop, with greater intensity and awareness, the relationship of reciprocity and the close bond that exist between the role of the diaconate and the overall mission of the Church and between the model of the diaconate to be pursued and the model of Church to strive toward tirelessly, while emphasizing, not only that the presence of the diaconate can facilitate a more lively and fruitful Church experience, but also that the diaconate produces its best results within a context of pastoral projects marked by co-responsibility in which the ordained ministry is called to animate and guide—not replace—the vivacity of the impulses that the Spirit arouses in the People of God.

---

129  Cf. Ugo Falesiedi, *Le Diaconie: I Servizi Assistenziali nella Chiesa Antica* (Rome: Institutum Patristicum Augustinianum, 1995).

# The Words of Cardinal Bergoglio

## Speech Given at the CELAM Fifth *Aparecida* Conference

The process of secularization tends to reduce the faith of the Catholic Church to the sphere of intimacy. Secularism, by continuing to reject the Transcendent, has produced a growing deterioration of ethics, a destabilization of the sense of sin, and a steady increase in moral relativism. This has led to a general sense of disorientation, especially in the periods of adolescence and young adulthood, moments that are so vulnerable and inclined to change.

The documents in *Pastoral Guidelines for the New Evangelization* from 1990 marked two great challenges: secularism as a phenomenon that "directly attacks faith and religion so as to neglect God" and "long-awaited justice." This has grave consequences for social life: by excluding God, man is stripped of his last point of reference, and his values are emptied of their essential content and transform into idols that enslave and degrade him. The second topic is justice: Argentinians are presented with the challenge of overcoming injustice and building a nation of brothers united by solidarity and shared sacrifice.

Three years after that document, the situation worsened and the bishops presented only one challenge in the document *Navega Mar Adentro*, the crisis of civilization and culture. From here, four more aspects emerged in relation to this crisis: "the search for God," "the scandal of poverty and social exclusion," "the crisis of marriage and the family," "the need for greater communion." This certainly did not mean for the bishops that the challenges connected to the problems that were revealed previously had disappeared or been resolved. Indeed, "secularism" is intertwined with the scandal of social poverty and exclusion. The radical and totalizing challenge we are facing is the profound crisis of cultural values.

Despite all of the secularism in our country, the Catholic Church enjoys positive public opinion and remains a credible and reliable institution with regards to solidarity and its concern for the great lack that exists. The experiences of ecumenical dialogue and the work done with historic churches and various evangelical communities are promising, especially in the prospective of being able to accompany communities through critical and difficult moments created by the economic crisis that spread into the plane of social coexistence. During the crisis that hit the country in 2001, the Catholic Church played an important part in participating in and supporting dialogue with the city. This demonstrates its reliability, the product of its freedom from any kind of partisanship or ideology. In recent years, the number of structures of communion has increased through joint pastoral plans, pastoral assemblies and diocesan synods. Despite the irreligiousness that reigns in parishes, the response coming from suburban chapels and basic communities of deacons, religious men and women, and the laity, are the guarantee of a place for communion, participation, and socialization, authentic evangelization, and the catechesis and experience of lay ministries.

*Aparecida*, May 30, 2007

# *Aparecida* Message to Priests

## *Challenges for Priests and Requests from the People of God*

As I have already mentioned, the *Aparecida* document refers to situations that affect and challenge the lives of our priests. The document touches upon the theological identity of the ministry of priests and their introduction into particular situations that are part of life today. You can read about this in the previous numbers. Here, I would like to focus on what the People of God ask of their priests, as listed in number 199 of the document. Five characteristics stand out: (a) that they have a deep experience of God, configuring their hearts to that of the Good Shepherd, they are docile to the motions of the

Spirit, and that they are nourished by the Word of God, the Eucharist, and prayer; (b) for missionary-priests: who are moved by pastoral charity that leads them to care for the flock entrusted to them and to seek out who have strayed furthest . . . ; (c) that they are in deep communion with their bishop, other priests, deacons, men and women religious, and lay people; d) for servant-of-life-priests: who are alert to the needs of the poorest, committed to the defense of the rights of the weakest, and promoters of the culture of solidarity; (e) full of mercy, available to administer the Sacrament of Mercy. Growing and preserving this priestly identity requires "a ministry for priests that emphasizes the specific spirituality and permanent and specific formation of priests."

Brochero, September 11, 2008

# The Meaning and Importance of Academic Formation

## *Formation for a Fullness of Life*

All of formation is aimed at forming good pastors who are capable of communicating the fullness of life of Jesus Christ to our people, as the *Aparecida* document asks:

"The People of God feel the need for disciple-priests: those who have a deep experience of God, are configured to the heart of the Good Shepherd, docile to the motions of the Spirit, who are nourished by the Word of God, the Eucharist and prayer; for missionary-priests: who are moved by pastoral charity which leads them to care for the flock entrusted to them and to seek out who have strayed furthest, preaching the Word of God, always in deep communion with their bishop, priests, deacons, men and women religious, and lay people; for servant-of-life-priests: who are alert to the needs of the poorest, committed to the defense of the rights of the weakest, and promoters of the culture of solidarity. The need is also for priests full of mercy, available to administer the sacrament of Reconciliation."[130]

The *Aparecida* document formulates these characteristics of priestly identity with a literary style that reflects what the People of God ask of their priests. Our faithful want "pastors of the people," not "state functionaries." They want "teachers of life" who teach the solid doctrine that saves, not "amateurs" committed to defending their own fame and discussing matters of lesser importance. Being good pastors and teachers who communicate life requires a deep and solid spirituality of communion with Christ the Shepherd and docility to the motions of the Spirit from the very beginning of formation.

Rome, February 18, 2009

---

130 Latin American Episcopal Conference, *Aparecida* Document, Fifth General Conference of the Bishops of Latin America and the Caribbean, no. 199.

# Pope Francis

# PART VI

# Deacons as Dispensers of Charity

When Pope Francis was first elected, he sent Msgr. Joaquín Sucunza, the auxiliary bishop of Buenos Aires, a handwritten letter to be read aloud at the end of the celebration of the Ordination of Deacons in the cathedral.

In this letter, Pope Francis uses the expression "put flesh to fire" in reference to Deacon Lawrence, who, tradition has it, was burned over a gridiron.

He was the first deacon in Rome, and he had the task of distributing to the poor what was collected from the city's Christians. Tradition has passed down to us the events surrounding his death, about how he met Pope Sixtus II, who was led to martyrdom, about how he refused to hand over the Church's "treasure" that had been entrusted to him, and about how he suffered the torture of the gridiron, which then became his iconic motif.

"The Roman Church," says St. Augustine, "commends this day [August 10] to us as the blessed Lawrence's day of triumph, on which he trod down the world as it roared and raged against him. How glorious a wreath is worn by Lawrence the martyr, and with what a multitude of virtues it is adorned, as with a variety of flowers, the whole city of Rome can testify.

"It was in that Church, you see, as you have regularly been told, that he performed the office of deacon; there that he administered the sacred chalice of Christ's Blood; there that he shed his own blood for the name of Christ. He loved Christ in his life, he imitated him in his death."[131]

Augustine summarized the most important aspects of St. Lawrence's life in these brief words. Augustine attended the beautifully celebrated anniversary of the saint martyr many times in Rome.[132] Indeed, like the saint Apostles, St. Lawrence had the privilege of a solemn Vigil in memory of the glorious night that he was martyred.

During the High Medieval Period, on August 10, one Mass was celebrated on Lawrence's tomb and another, more solemn Mass was celebrated in the Basilica of St. Lawrence Outside the Walls (San Lorenzo in Damaso), which was built by Constantine. There was an inscription inside the basilica at that time that is considered to be the oldest historical account of St. Lawrence:

> The whips of his executioners, the flames, the tortures, the chains,
> Lawrence's faith alone could overcome them.

---

131 St. Augustine, *Sermon* 304, On the Feast Day of Lawrence the Martyr, no. 1. English translation from *The Works of Saint Augustine: A Translation for the 21st Century*, Vol. 8, Sermons 273-305A (Hyde Park, New York: New City Press/Augustinian Heritage Institute) 316.

132 St. Augustine, *Sermon* 303, no.1.

Damasus, suppliant, fill these altars with gifts
Admiring the merits of the glorious martyr.[133]

Despite the brevity of this inscription, it is of particular interest for how old it is. It was written by St. Damasus about a century after St. Lawrence's death. Legend soon surrounded this extraordinary death; even St. Ambrose referenced some of the events. As for St. Augustine, he always takes certain oratory precautions when recounting the circumstances surrounding the life and martyrdom of St. Lawrence.

St. Lawrence was one of the seven deacons of Rome under Pope Sixtus II (258). For a long time, the number of deacons in Rome was limited to seven, one for each ecclesiastical region. In addition to the ministry of the altar and assisting the pope, Roman deacons were in charge administering the temporal goods of the Roman Church. This function made deacons important figures within the Church, and it often happened that popes were chosen from among the deacons instead of from among the priests.

Since he belonged to the hierarchy of the Church, St. Lawrence was subject to Valerian's edict, dated 258. The act ordered the capital execution of any bishop, priest, or deacon who could be identified. St. Sixtus was struck by the persecution; he was arrested and

---

133 A. Ferrua, *Epigramma Damasiana* (Vatican City, 1942), p. 177.

decapitated while celebrating the Liturgy in the cemetery of Callistus. Around that same time, six deacons were killed.

And so, St. Lawrence was the only one left, but he, too, did not have long to wait to bear witness to Christ in blood.

In this case, the persecutors had reason to be interested: St. Lawrence was, in fact, the only remaining steward of the Roman Church's goods. According to St. Ambrose, St. Lawrence was ordered to hand over the Church's treasures. After three days of hesitation, the deacon presented the judge not with silver and gold, but with the all of the poor people who had received his charity. St. Augustine concluded with: "The needs of the needy are the great wealth and treasure of Christians."[134]

Will this episode suffice to explain that St. Lawrence was tortured three days after St. Sixtus? He was handed over to his executioners on the night between August 9 and 10. With "firm faith" and "unshaken courage,"[135] St. Lawrence suffered the terrible torture of fire. It is true that "the refinement of cruelty involved in slowly burning the patient over a gridiron was contrary to Roman tradition." But no tradition holds when the passion of riches has corrupted the conscience of a judge, and, as a general principle, it would be hard to reject a fact that

---

134 St. Augustine, *Sermon* 302, no. 8.

135 St. Augustine, *Sermon* 296, no. 5.

is so easily explained by the circumstances explained above. Torture with fire was also used Lyon in 177. Lastly, we have St. Damasus's account of St. Lawrence that was mentioned earlier. The importance of this epigram is undoubtedly minimized, given its "enumeration of classic tortures." However, there is another inscription in San Lorenzo in Damaso, which was going to be discarded because it is "impossible to date," but which, according to a contemporary Roman archeologist, is very old and very likely from Pope Damasus himself.

It is with faith, the text says, that Lawrence overcame the torture of the flames through which the path to heaven passes.

St. Augustine attributes St. Lawrence's victory to his eminent charity: "Placed on a gridiron, he was scorched all over his body, tortured with the most excruciating pains by fire. Yet he overcame all these bodily afflictions with the sturdy strength of his charity."[136]

At the same time, the Holy Doctor gives us a glimpse into what were to be the martyr's last moments: "Temporal life is extinguished, but eternal life if obtained instead. What an honor and what an assurance it is to go hence joyfully, to go out gloriously amid affliction and distress; to shut in a moment the eyes men and the

---

136 St. Augustine, *Sermon 302, On the Birthday of St. Lawrence* (Date: 400), no. 8.

world are seen with, and to open them immediately to see God!"[137]

## He Administered the Blood of Christ

From the *Sermons* of
St. Augustine, Bishop[138]

The Roman Church commends this day to us as the blessed Lawrence's day of triumph, on which he trod down the world as it roared and raged against him, spurned it as it coaxed and wheedled him, and in each case conquered the devil as he persecuted him. . . . It was in that Church, you see, as you have regularly been told, that he performed the office of deacon; there that he administered the sacred chalice of Christ's blood; there that he shed his own blood for the name of Christ. . . .

The blessed apostle John clearly explained the mystery of this dinner when he said, "Just as Christ laid down his life for us, so we too ought to lay down our lives for the brethren" (1 Jn 3:16). St. Lawrence understood this, brothers and sisters, and he did it; and he undoubtedly prepared things similar to what

---

137 St. Augustine, *Sermon 303, On the Birthday of the Martyr Lawrence* (Date: 426), no. 2.

138 St. Augustine, *Sermon 304, On the Feast Day of Lawrence the Martyr* (Date: 417), nos. 1-3.

he received at that table. He loved Christ in his life, he imitated him in his death.

And we too, brothers and sisters, if we truly love him, let us imitate him. After all, we won't be able to give a better proof of love than by imitating him. "For Christ suffered for us, leaving us an example, so that we might follow in his footsteps" (1 Pt 2:21). In this sentence the apostle Peter appears to have seen that Christ suffered only for those who follow in his footsteps, and that Christ's passion profits none but those who follow in his footsteps. The holy martyrs followed him, to the shedding of their blood, to the similarity of their sufferings. The martyrs followed, but they were not the only ones. It's not the case, I mean to say, that after they had crossed, the bridge was cut; or that after they had drunk, the fountain dried up. . . .

That garden of the Lord's, brothers and sisters, includes, yes it includes, it certainly includes not only the roses of martyrs, but also the lilies of virgins, and the ivy of married people, and the violets of widows. There is absolutely no kind of human beings, dearly beloved, who need to despair of their vocation; Christ suffered for all. It was very truly written about him: "who wishes all men to be saved, and to come to the acknowledgment of the truth" (1 Tm 2:4).

So let us understand how Christians ought to follow Christ, short of the shedding of blood, short of the danger of suffering death. The apostle says, speaking of the Lord Christ, "Who, though he was in the form of God, did not think it robbery to be equal to God." What incomparable greatness! "But he emptied himself, taking the form of a servant, and being made in the likeness of men, and found in condition as a man." What unequalled humility! Christ humbled himself; you have something, Christian, to latch on to. Christ "became obedient." Why do you behave proudly? . . .

After running the course of these humiliations, and laying death low, Christ ascended into heaven; let us follow him there. Let us listen to the apostle telling us, "If you have risen with Christ, savor the things that are above where Christ is, seated at God's right hand" (Col 3:1).

# [Transcript][139]

In his *De Officiis* (1, ch. 41, no. 205-207), we have Ambrose's particularly eloquent account of the martyrdom of St. Lawrence. . . .

Ambrose dwells, firstly on the encounter and dialogue between Lawrence and Sixtus. He alludes

---

139 Fr. Francesco Moraglia, "St. Lawrence: Proto-Deacon of the Roman Church," February 19, 2000, Vatican Congregation of the Clergy, Holy Year 2000 - Jubilee for Permanent Deacons. *www.vatican.va/roman_curia/congregations/cclergy/documents/ rc_con_cclergy_doc_19022000_slaw_en.htmlm.*

to the distribution of the Church's goods to the poor and mentions the gridiron, the instrument of Lawrence's torture and remarks on the words that the proto-Deacon of the Roman Church addresses to his torturers: *assum est, . . . versa et manduca* (cf. Bibliotheca Sanctorum, vol. I, col. 1538-1539).

We shall dwell on the Ambrosian text of the *De Officiis* (ch. 41, nos. 205-207), which is so very moving in its intensity and strength of expression. Thus writes St. Ambrose:

> St. Lawrence wept when he saw his Bishop, Sixtus, led out to his martyrdom. He wept not because he was being let out to die but because he would survive Sixtus. He cried out to him in a loud voice: "Where are you going Father, without your son? Where do you hasten to, holy Bishop, without your Deacon? You cannot offer sacrifice without a minister. Father, are you displeased with something in me? Do you think me unworthy? Show us a sign that you have found a worthy minister. Do you not wish that he to whom you gave the Lord's blood and with whom you have shared the sacred mysteries should spill his own blood with you? Beware that in your praise your own judgment should not falter. Despise the pupil and shame the Master. Do not forget that great and famous men are victorious

more in the deeds of their disciples than in their own. Abraham made sacrifice of his own son, Peter instead sent Stephen. Father, show us your own strength in your sons; sacrifice him whom you have raised, to attain eternal reward in that glorious company, secure in your judgment.

In reply, Sixtus says: "I will not leave you, I will not abandon you my son. More difficult trials are kept for you. A shorter race is set for us who are older. For you who are young a more glorious triumph over tyranny is reserved. Soon, you will see, cry no more, after three days you will follow me. It is fitting that such an interval should be set between Bishop and Levite. It would not have been fitting for you to die under the guidance of a martyr, as though you needed help from him. Why do want to share in my martyrdom? I leave its entire inheritance to you. Why do need me present? The weak pupil precedes the master, the strong, who have no further need of instruction, follow and conquer without him. Thus Elijah left Elisha. I entrust the success of my strength to you."

This was the contest between them which was worthy of a Bishop and of a Deacon: who would be the first to die for Christ. . . . Neither of these deserved to live for both were guilty of patricide. One because he had killed his father, the other because he had been an accomplice in patricide. In the case of Lawrence, nothing urged him to offer himself as a victim but the desire to be a holocaust for Christ. Three days after the death of Sixtus, while the terror raged, Lawrence would be burned on the gridiron: "'This side is done, turn and eat.' With such strength of soul he conquered the flames of the fire."[140]

According to Ambrose, the Deacon is one who

1. Having been sacramentally constituted in the service of offering (*diakonia*), lives his diaconal ministry giving supreme witness to Christ in martyrdom—the theological meaning of the service of charity by acceptance of that greater love or charity which is martyrdom;

2. In virtue of the structural link which binds him to the Bishop (the first stage of Orders), lives 'ecclesial communion' by specific service to the Bishop, beginning with the Eucharist and in reference to the Eucharist;

3. In virtue of the Sacrament (that is, to the extent that he is rooted in the first grade of Orders), devotes himself totally to the service of an integral charity and

---

140 Cfr. St. Ambrose, *De Officiis*, *libri tres*, Milan, Biblioteca Ambrosiana (Rome: Città Nuova Editrice 1977) 148-151.

not merely to a human or social solidarity, and thereby manifests the most characteristic element of the diaconia.

. . . The Deacon is one who having been sacramentally constituted in the service of offering (*diakonia*), lives his diaconal ministry giving supreme witness to Christ in martyrdom—the theological meaning of the service of charity by acceptance of that greater love or charity which is martyrdom.

The principle characteristic defining the Deacon . . . is that he is ordained for the service of charity. Martyrdom, which is a witness to the point of shedding one's blood, must be considered an expression of greater love or charity. It is service to a charity that knows no limits. The ministry of charity in which the Deacon is deputed by ordination is not limited to service at table, or indeed to what former catechetical terminology called corporal works of mercy, nor to the spiritual works of mercy. The diaconal service of charity must include imitation of Christ by means of unconditional self-giving since he is the fruitful witness (cf. Rev 1:5; 3:14).

# The Words of Pope Francis

*Dearest Sons and Brothers,*

It would have given me so much joy to be there with you today! There is no doubt that I am there in spirit. You have just received the diaconate and publicly manifested your vocation to service . . . and this is not only for a period of time but for all your life. May your priestly existence be a service: service for Jesus Christ, service for the Church, and service to brothers, especially the poorest and those most in need. Don't be "part-time deacons" or functionaries. The Church is not an NGO. May service enhance your lives. "Put flesh to fire." I am praying for each of you, for your desires and your sufferings. And do not forget that Jesus has been watching over you; keep letting Jesus watch over you. Please, pray for me. May Jesus Christ bless you and may the Virgin Mary protect you!

Fondly,

Francis

Vatican City, March 13, 2013

## Homily at Santa Marta

A humble Church that does not show off her powers, her grandeur. Humility doesn't mean a lethargic, weary person with a demure expression. . . . No, this is not humility, this is theatrics! This is feigned humility. True humility begins with the first step: "I am a sinner." If you are not able to tell yourself that you are a sinner and that others are better than you, you are not humble. The first step for a humble Church is feeling that she is a sinner and the same is true for all of us. If any of us has the habit of looking at others' defects and gossiping, this is not humility. It is thinking that you are the judge of others. . . . Our deacon, the deacon of this diocese, Deacon Lawrence—the "treasurer of the diocese"—who, when the emperor asked him to bring the riches of the diocese to turn them over in order to avoid being killed, St. Lawrence returned with the poor. The poor are the treasure of the Church. You can even be the head of a bank, as long as your heart is poor, not attached to money and you place yourself at the service of others.

Where do I place my trust? In power, in friends, in money? In the Lord! It is this legacy that the Lord promises us: "I will leave in the midst of you a people humble and lowly. They shall seek refuge in the name of the Lord." Humble because they feel they are sinners; poor because their heart is attached to God's treasures, and if they have them it is only to administer them; seeking refuge in the Lord because they know that the Lord alone can guarantee what is good for them. This is why Jesus had to tell the chief priests, who did not understand these things, that a harlot would enter the Kingdom of God before them.

Tuesday, December 15, 2015

# PART VII

# The Deacon in the Church, People of God

[Transcript]¹⁴¹

Diaconia is more than just a collection of knowledge and experiences, it is a way of life. For this reason, it requires a fundamental option that has an eschatological end: the hope of new life and the Kingdom of God as the focal point and direction for one's life. An objective only has meaning when it is pursued with faith, hope, and charity. J. Moltmann wrote: "The world is a testing ground for the kingdom of God. Love can only be practiced if the systems that create competition, hate, and war are eliminated, and if the 'new order of things'¹⁴² and peace are brought in. Diaconia, in this case, is not only the alleviating

---

141 Prof. Ludwig Schmidt, lecturer at the Center for Religious Studies of the Catholic University of Caracas (Venezuela), "Perspectives for the Formation of Deacons in the Ministry," Symposium on the Formation of Deacons, Heligkreuztal (Germany), Sept. 11-17, 2000. Unofficial English translation. Originally published in Italian as *"Prospettive per la formazione dei diaconi al minister,"* cached version of the Italian text: *http://webcache.googleusercontent.com/search?q=cache:y7kEhpuP4qY-J:www.dehoniane.it:9080/komodo/trunk/webapp/web/files/r* (accessed May 1, 2018).

142 Jürgen Moltmann, *Théologie de l'esperance*, p. 25.

of suffering, the healing of wounds, and the supplying of social compensations, but it is the anticipation of new life, new community, and the world of freedom. Diaconia is not directed only toward man's present pain, but also toward the Kingdom of God, the true future of humanity. Without the prospect of the Kingdom of God, diaconia is nothing else than love without ideas that only knows how to compensate. But, without diaconia, hope for the Kingdom of God becomes a utopia without love that only knows how to make demands and accuse. So, in diaconal practice, a relationship must be created between love and hope, between the Kingdom of God and concrete needs."[143]

Jesus Christ himself, the servant and Good Samaritan, is the starting point from which we can begin interpreting the "ministeriality of the Church." Jesus of Nazareth placed his life at the service of men (cf. Mk 10:43-45; Mt 10:24) to such an extent that he did not hesitate to wash the feet of his Apostles at the Last Supper (cf. Jn 13:3-20) and to serve them food. He suffered and gave his life as ransom for humanity (cf. Mk 15:33-39; Mt 27:45-54; Lk 23:44-47; Jn 19:28-30), so as to then triumphantly resurrect from the dead and let each of us share in his

---

143 Jürgen Moltmann, *Diaconia*, 25.

life (cf. Jn 3:16), in the end becoming a paradigm of life on the pilgrim journey from Galilee.

The Church, which carries on the salvific action of Jesus Christ, also becomes the subject of the proclamation of the message inculturated and incarnated in her people and of the promotion of the salvific paradigm of her Master through her mission and service. In this sense, the Church will have to be understood in her "ministeriality" in the place where all baptized men and women have become potential followers of his love and servants of brothers in Jesus Christ so that, inspired by the obedience to the Father, they exercise their roles and by the power of the Holy Spirit, they express the many gifts that have been given to them (cf. 1 Cor 12:4-7). The specific character of the Christian community is completely determined by its faith in Jesus, the Living Christ who, through the Spirit, calls all people to him and in him.

The truest seal of the Christian vocation is service; a service of faith, in hope and with charity. It is a ministry that must shine in conformity with the dignity of being ministers of Christ. Therefore, this service is completely removed from any kind of competition over positions to hold or power; it is service that helps without ulterior motives, like a "Good Samaritan in Judea," and without ever asking, "Who is my neighbor?" In the Church of the Lord, first place and true greatness are reserved for those who serve, for the servant of Yahweh and his people, for the minister who is willing to give his life for the "other" without expecting anything in return.

With his charism of service to charity, the deacon listens to the cries of the needs of the poor, of those who suffer, and of the humble, cries that always make their way to the Church. It is through this action that the Gospel must be realized, it must be understood and assimilated, it must transform (*metànoia*), it must remain valid, and it must be fulfilled "today" (cf. Lk 4:21); because "yesterday, as today," Jesus' indefectible word is always with the poor who are in constant need of this service. Because we will "always" (cf. Mt 26:11) have the poor with us.

# Deacons at the Service of the People of God

The diaconate has come a long way since its reintroduction in reflecting on its identity and gaining gradual awareness. The predominantly pastoral Second Vatican Council, with its ecclesiology of communion centered on *Lumen Gentium*, unequivocally decided for the diaconal ministry[144] to be brought back into the Church as

---

144 Second Vatican Ecumenical Council, Dogmatic Constitution on the Church *Lumen Gentium* (LG), no. 29.

its own ministry, and not just as a stop along the way to becoming a priest. It is a ministry which can be conferred upon celibates and married men alike. The restoration of the diaconate as a rank of the hierarchy is highlighted by the "imposition of hands" and "sacramental grace," which underline the sacramentality of the diaconate. The conciliar text affirms that the service of Bishops[145] is exercised with the help of priests and deacons. It further emphasizes that the divinely established *ecclesiastical ministry* has been exercised since antiquity on different levels by bishops, priests, and deacons.[146]

In two different Wednesday General Audiences, Pope Francis affirms that "in the ministry of the bishops, of the priests and deacons, we can recognize the true face of the Church: it is the Hierarchical Holy Mother Church." He also states that "no Church is healthy if the faithful, the deacons and the priests are not united to the bishop. This Church, that is not united to the bishop, is a sick Church."[147]

The diaconate, as Paul VI said, was restored as a *factor in the renewal of the Church*, a statement that intended to open new horizons for the diaconal ministry by helping it overcome the ever-present danger of falling into *neoritualism* or *neodevotionism*: the *dignity* of the *People*

---

145  LG, no. 30.

146  LG, no. 28.

147  Pope Francis, General Audience (November 5, 2014).

*of God* must be understood and made to emerge in an ever more effective way so as to better understand the specific nature of the vocation to the diaconate and of every ministry in general.

Moreover, the aim of the formula adopted by the Council, that is, "not unto the priesthood, but unto a ministry of service,"[148] which is an adaptation of traditional patristic and liturgical thought, is to clarify that even though the deacon participates in his degree of the ministerial priesthood, he is not, however, ordained to consecrate the Body and Blood of Christ or—as a general rule—to preside over the liturgical assembly; he is ordained *to service of the bishop, priests, and the Christian people*. As we have learned from many Church Fathers (especially St. Ignatius of Antioch), the deacon had a very important role in the early Church up until the fifth century. He fulfilled his service by letting it flow directly and primarily from the Eucharist, thereby highlighting Jesus' service of charity that washes the feet of brothers and that the Eucharist is the point of arrival of all Christian service. In the *Didascalia of the Apostles*, we read that deacons must work in close and cordial communion with the bishop, for whom they must be the "hearing, mouth, heart, and soul: both of one mind."[149] This expression is very important for its ecclesial and

---

148 LG, no. 29.

149 *Didascalia of the Apostles*, Ch. XVI.

pastoral value and, especially, for the identity and service of deacons today. It shows that deacons are ordained to collaborate with the bishop, and therefore, for the local Church.

Moreover, the deacon's relationship with the laity comes from the fact that, through sacramental grace, he is able to recognize their many needs and to bring about services and ministries in the People of God. The deacon's position at the service of the People of God means that, while he has received an ordination and is, therefore, part of the clergy, he also shares the life of the laity who support him as one of their own.

As part of the Sacrament of Holy Orders, the ministry of the deacon has a kind authority among the faithful that is similar to that of the priest, but at the same time, since the deacon is a part of the common condition of the people, he shares and understands their problems and helps priests understand them as well.

The excessively dynamic and, at times, alienating rhythm of our society and our Church communities undoubtedly dehumanizes our direct and personal contact with the people, reducing it to a chaotic encounter of secondary relationships with no points of contact or opportunities for the vital exchange of experiences and collaboration.

These difficulties are also present in our parishes where our communities are moving toward faceless anonymity, toward predominantly mass, and sometimes only formal, encounters that are devoid of personal human contact. It is a crisis of communication because people today no longer turn to the parish to receive adequate formation. The only moment priests have to reach their faithful is during Sunday Mass, and it is a moment that leaves little room for spontaneous and constructive dialogue.

In this sense, the diaconate and its exercise must be seen in relation to a Church that grows in the awareness of her missionary existence. It is a commitment that must push pastoral work beyond the mere preservation of the present and courageously open it up to the new demands of society.

Finally, Francis focuses on what the Apostle Paul writes about the qualities that ordained ministers must have: "It is emblematic that, along with the gifts inherent in the faith and in spiritual life . . . some exquisitely human qualities are listed: acceptance, temperance, patience, meekness, trustworthiness, goodness of heart. This is the alphabet, the basic grammar, of every ministry! It must be the basic grammar of every bishop, priest and deacon."[150]

Here, a profound and radical challenge appears. The last twenty years have seen profound changes internationally as well as here in Italy, especially in the south. Our relationship with the eastern and southern shores of

---

150  Pope Francis, General Audience (November 12, 2014).

the Mediterranean is no longer the same. Mass immigration from Eastern Europe, Africa, and Asia has created the urgent need for new forms of solidarity. The south of Italy is very often the first landing place of hope for thousands of immigrants, and it serves as an ecclesial workshop where, after reception, aid, and hospitality are secured, an attempt is made at Christian discernment, at a journey toward justice and human promotion, and at an encounter with the religions professed by immigrants and refugees.

As the document highlights, the historic changes affecting the societies of our time and the current ecclesial situation must push us to mature a diaconal profile that is new, to a certain extent, and that comes from the identification and implementation of potentialities of service required by a social fabric, such as that of today, which is all too often dominated by interests and torn apart by compromise and the abuse of power. In fact, it is here, among people who work, suffer, and search for meaning, that deacons are called to witness the spirit of the Beatitudes and, through their presence, to reveal the Christ of a new world, a world that has yet to be built. Today, Pope Francis says, we want to ask ourselves: "What is asked of these ministers of the Church, in order that they may live out their service in a genuine and fruitful way?"[151]

---

151 General Audience (November 12, 2014).

This provocation must help us understand the relationship of reciprocity and the close bond that exist between the role of the diaconate and the overall mission of the Church and between the model of the diaconate to be pursued and the model of Church to strive toward tirelessly, while emphasizing, not only that the presence of the diaconate can facilitate a more lively and fruitful Church experience, but also the other way around.

Deacons are also called to live in symbiosis with the people and near the people, in close proximity to their happy and sad family events, with a willingness to listen and to embrace those in hardship, with the willingness to visit them in their homes. Deacons are being asked more and more frequently by parish priests to bless families during the Easter period where they live. The word "people," like the word "world," is full of ambivalence, and its meaning can only be specified by its context. The Gospels tell of Jesus' compassion for people. It is interesting, then, to take Jesus' question to his disciples seriously: "Who do people say that I am?" (Mk 8:27). Thus, it is not at all innocuous to ask ourselves how people see us. Honest scrutiny of the discrepancy between what people see and what we deeply feel to be, could force us to seriously rethink who we are, our faith, and our ministry. It is a stimulating litmus test.

It is essential and urgent, therefore, that we, as deacons, evaluate the service that we have offered the Christian community and the world in the post-conciliar years so that we can understand how we have contributed to expanding the horizons of the diaconia of Christ to the entire life and mission of the Church in our time, and to understand whether a "diaconal conscience," that is, an awareness of diaconia that translates into participation and co-responsibility at all levels and in all its different forms, has matured in our communities because of our actions. There is another statement that challenges us and that can only be answered with our life of ministry. Francis addressed everyone, saying, "Go out into the streets and go out to the crossroads: call all those whom you find, excluding no one (cf. Mt 22:9). Accompany especially those who are on the roadside, 'the lame, the maimed, the blind, the dumb' (Mt 15:30). Wherever you may be, build neither walls nor borders but village squares and field hospitals."[152] The pope's words offer a particular indication for deacons, the great task of our time, which is marked by the creativity and the challenges that are typical of every epochal change. When new challenges arise, especially challenges that are difficult to understand, the instinctive reaction is to withdraw, to defend oneself, to build walls and establish impassable boundaries.

This reaction is human, too human. Nevertheless, deacons must avoid this risk to the extent that they become truly aware of their diaconia, not only in the

---

152 Pope Francis, Address to Participants in the Fifth Convention of the Italian Church (November 10, 2015).

Church, but in the world, in and through the change and the challenges. And so, a new perspective unfolds for the diaconal ministry: it can "go forth" with confidence, it finds the courage to walk along the streets of man, it has the strength to build village squares and to offer the company of care and mercy to those who have been left on the side of the road. This is Pope Francis's "dream" for the men and women who must witness Christ. It is up to us to put our hearts, hands, and heads into making this "dream" a reality. It is essential to recognize that *"going forth" is more of a movement than a tool; it is not a specific activity among others, but a "style,"* or rather, the unifying form of the life of the deacon and of the Church as a whole. As the pope remarked, "Christian humanity always goes forth. It is not narcissistic or self-referential."[153]

Without ecclesial growth, the service of deacons risks being misunderstood and becoming a kind of "commissioned" commitment that, as a result of choices inspired or dictated by urgency, is devoted to resolving the passing needs and occasional logistical problems of individual churches. Unfortunately, this has often happened. Diaconia according to the conciliar model, on the other hand, is the re-proposing of the "new commandment" that Christ gave to his disciples. In this context, the witness of diaconal service is destined to

---

153 Address (November 10, 2015).

become the historical sign, thereby becoming able pay close attention to mankind and to the signs of the times.

# The Words of Pope Francis

## Audiences

*Dear Brothers and Sisters,*

We have already had occasion to point out that the three Sacraments of Baptism, Confirmation and the Eucharist together constitute the mystery of "Christian initiation," a single great event of grace that regenerates us in Christ. This is the fundamental vocation which unites everyone in the Church as disciples of the Lord Jesus. There are then two Sacraments which correspond to two specific vocations: Holy Orders and Matrimony. They constitute two great paths by which the Christian can make his life a gift of love, after the example and in the name of Christ, and thus cooperate in the building up of the Church.

Holy Orders, in its three grades of bishop, priest and deacon, is the Sacrament that enables a man to exercise the ministry which the Lord Jesus entrusted to the Apostles, to shepherd his flock, in the power of his Spirit and according to his Heart. Tending Jesus' flock not by the power of human strength or by one's own power, but by the Spirit's and according to his Heart, the Heart of Jesus which is a heart of love. The priest, the bishop, the deacon must shepherd the Lord's flock with love. It is useless if it is not done with love. And in this sense, the ministers who are chosen and consecrated for this service extend Jesus' presence in time, if they do so by the power of the Holy Spirit, in God's name and with love.

1. A first aspect. Those who are ordained are placed *at the head of the community*. They are "at the head," yes, but for Jesus this means placing one's authority *at the service* [of the community], as Jesus himself showed and taught his disciples with these words: "You know that the rulers of the Gentiles lord it over them, and their great men exercise authority over them. It shall not be so among you; but whoever would be great among you must be your servant, and whoever would be first among you must be your slave; even as the Son of man came not to be served but to serve, and to give his life as a ransom for many" (Mt 20:25-28; Mk 10:42-45). A bishop who is not at the service of the community fails to perform his duty; a priest who is not at the service of his community fails to perform his duty, he errs.

2. Another characteristic which also derives from this sacramental union with Christ is a *passionate love for the Church*. Let us think of that passage from the Letter to the Ephesians in which St. Paul states that Christ "loved the Church and gave himself up for her, that he might sanctify her, having cleansed her by the washing of water with the word, that he might present the Church to himself in splendor, without spot or wrinkle or any such thing" (5:25-27). Through Holy Orders the minister (the deacon) dedicates himself entirely to his

143

community and loves it with all his heart: it is his family. The bishop and the priest love the Church in their own community, they love it greatly. How? As Christ loves the Church. St. Paul will say the same of marriage: the husband is to love his wife as Christ loves the Church. It is a great mystery of love: this of priestly ministry and that of matrimony are two Sacraments, pathways which people normally take to go to the Lord.

3. A final aspect. The Apostle Paul recommends to the disciple Timothy that he not neglect, indeed, that he always rekindle the gift that is within him. The gift that he has been given through the laying on of hands (cf. 1 Tm 4:14; 2 Tm 1:6).

Wednesday, March 26, 2014

## Holy Mother Church as Hierarchy

*Dear Brothers and Sisters, Good morning,*

We have listened to what the Apostle Paul says to Bishop Tito. How many virtues do we bishops have? We heard everything, did we not? It's not easy, it's not easy, because we are sinners. But we entrust ourselves to your prayers, so that we may at least come closer to these things that the Apostle Paul advises all bishops. Do you agree? Will you pray for us?

We have already had the occasion to stress, in preceding catecheses, how the Holy Spirit is always abundantly filling the Church with his gifts. Now, by the power and grace of His Spirit, Christ does not fail to set up ministries in order to build up Christian communities as his Body. Among these ministries, one can distinguish that of the episcopate. In the bishop, assisted by priests and deacons, it is Christ himself who makes himself present and who continues to care for his Church, by ensuring his protection and his guidance.

1. In the presence and in the ministry of the bishops, of the priests and deacons, we can recognize the true face of the Church: it is the Hierarchical Holy Mother Church. And truly, through these brothers chosen by the Lord and consecrated through the Sacrament of Holy Orders, the Church exercises her motherhood: she gives birth to us in Baptism as Christians, giving us a new birth in Christ; she watches over our growth in the faith; she accompanies us into the arms of the Father, to receive his forgiveness; she prepares the Eucharistic table for us, where she nourishes us with the Word of God and the Body and Blood of Jesus; she invokes upon us the blessing of God and the power of his Spirit, sustaining us throughout the course of our life and enveloping us with her tenderness and warmth, especially in those most delicate moments of trial, of suffering and of death.

2. This motherhood of the Church is expressed in particular in the person of the bishop and in his ministry. In fact, as Jesus chose the Apostles and sent them

out to proclaim the Gospel and to tend his flock, so bishops, his successors, are set at the head of Christian communities, as guarantors of the faith and as living signs of the presence of the Lord among them. We understand, then, that this is not a position of prestige, an honorary title. The episcopate is not an honor, it's a service. This is how Jesus wanted it. There should be no place in the Church for a worldly mentality. The worldly mentality says: "This man took the ecclesiastical career path, he became a bishop." No, no, in the Church there must be no place for this mindset. The episcopate is a service, not an honor to boast about. Being a bishop means keeping before one's eyes the example of Jesus who, as the Good Shepherd, came not to be served, but to serve (cf. Mt 20:28; Mk 10:45) and to give his life for his sheep (cf. Jn 10:11). Holy bishops—and there are many in the history of the Church, many holy bishops—show us that this ministry is not sought, is not requested, is not bought, but is accepted in obedience, not in order to elevate oneself, but to lower oneself, as Jesus did who "humbled himself and became obedient unto death, even death on a cross" (Phil 2:8). It is sad when one sees a man who seeks this office and who does so much just to get there; and when he gets there, he does not serve, he struts around, he lives only for his own vanity.

3. There is another precious element that deserves to be pointed out. When Jesus chose and called the Apostles, He did not think of them as separate from

one another, each one on his own, but together, because they were to stay with Him, united, like a single family. Furthermore, bishops also constitute one single College, gathered around the Pope, who is the guardian and guarantor of this profound communion that was so close to Jesus' heart and to his Apostles' too. How beautiful it is, then, when bishops, with the Pope, express this collegiality and always seek to be better servants to the faithful, better servants in the Church! We recently experienced it in the Assembly of the Synod on the Family. Just think of all the bishops spread around the world who, despite living in widely different places, cultures, sensibilities and traditions—one bishop said to me the other day that it takes him more than thirty hours by plane to come to Rome—they each feel part of the other and they become an expression of the intimate bond, in Christ, between their communities. And in the common prayer of the Church, all bishops place themselves together in listening to the Lord and to the Holy Spirit, paying profound attention to man and to the signs of the times (cf. Pastoral Constitution *Gaudium et Spes*, no. 4).

Dear friends, all this makes us understand that Christian communities recognize in the bishop a great gift, and are called to nourish a sincere and profound communion with him, beginning with the priests and deacons. No Church is healthy if the faithful, the deacons and the priests are not united to the bishop. This Church, that is not united to the bishop, is a sick Church.

Jesus wanted this union of all the faithful with the bishop, including the deacons and priests. And this they do aware that it is precisely in the bishop that the bond is made visible with each Church, with the Apostles and with all other communities, united to their bishops and the Pope in the one Church of the Lord Jesus, that is our Hierarchical Holy Mother Church. Thank you.

Wednesday, November 5, 2014

## The Characteristics of the Ministers of the Church

*Dear Brothers and Sisters, Good morning,*

In the preceding catechesis on the Church, we pointed out how the Lord continues to shepherd his flock through the ministry of bishops, assisted by priests and deacons. It is in them that Jesus makes himself present, in the power of his Spirit, and continues to serve the Church, nourishing within her faith, hope and the witness of love. These ministers are thus a great gift of the Lord for every Christian community and for the whole of the Church, as they are a living sign of the presence of his love.

Today we want to ask ourselves: What is asked of these ministers of the Church, in order that they may live out their service in a genuine and fruitful way.

1. In the "Pastoral Letters" sent to his disciples, Timothy and Titus, the Apostle Paul carefully pauses

on the figures of bishop, priest and deacon, also on the figures of the faithful, the elderly and young people. He pauses on a description of each state of a Christian in the Church, delineating for bishops, priests and deacons what they are called to and what prerogatives must be acknowledged in those chosen and invested with these ministries. Today it is emblematic that, along with the gifts inherent in the faith and in spiritual life—which cannot be overlooked, for they are life itself—some exquisitely human qualities are listed: acceptance, temperance, patience, meekness, trustworthiness, goodness of heart. This is the alphabet, the basic grammar, of every ministry! It must be the basic grammar of every bishop, priest and deacon. Yes, this beautiful and genuine predisposition is necessary to meet, understand, dialogue with, appreciate and relate to brothers in a respectful and sincere way—without this predisposition it is not possible to offer truly joyous and credible service and testimony.

2. There is also a basic conduct which Paul recommends to his disciples and, as a result, to all those who are called to pastoral ministry, be they bishops, priests, presbyters or deacons. The Apostle says that the gift which has been received must be continually rekindled (cf. 1 Tm 4:14; 2 Tm 1:6). This means that there must always be a profound awareness that one is not bishop, priest or deacon because he is more intelligent, worthier or better than other men; he is such only pursuant to a gift, a gift of love bestowed by God, through the power

of his Spirit, for the good of his people. This awareness is very important and constitutes a grace to ask for every day! Indeed, a Pastor who is cognizant that his ministry springs only from the heart of God can never assume an authoritarian attitude, as if everyone were at his feet and the community were his property, his personal kingdom.

3. The awareness that everything is a gift, everything is grace, also helps a Pastor not to fall into the temptation of placin himself at the center of attention and trusting only in himself. They are the temptations of vanity, pride, sufficiency, arrogance. There would be problems if a bishop, a priest or a deacon thought he knew everything, that he always had the right answer for everything and did not need anyone. On the contrary, awareness that he, as the first recipient of the mercy and compassion of God, should lead a minister of the Church to always be humble and sympathetic with respect to others. Also, in the awareness of being called to bravely guard the faith entrusted (cf. 1 Tm 6:20), he shall listen to the people. He is in fact cognizant of always having something to learn, even from those who may still be far from the faith and from the Church. With his confreres, then, all this must lead to taking on a new attitude marked by sharing, joint responsibility and communion.

Dear friends, we must always be grateful to the Lord, for in the person and in the ministry of bishops, priests and deacons, he continues to guide and shape his Church, making her grow along the path of holiness.

At the same time, we must continue to pray, that the Pastors of our communities can be living images of the communion and of the love of God.

Wednesday, November 12, 2014

# PART VIII

# Deacons as Meek and Humble Servants of Christ and Brothers

Deacons are apostles and servants of God's "agenda" in the way of "meekness" of Jesus. These are words from Pope Francis's homily from the Eucharistic celebration on the morning of the Jubilee of Deacons on Corpus Christi in the packed St. Peter's Square.

The deacon's vocation, better yet, his "ambition," Pope Francis states, "cannot differ from this: a servant for all, for the expected and the unexpected brother," "adaptable," flexible and available, even with his time, to accept and "make room for those in need." The deacon is not a "bureaucrat of the sacred with timetables that regulate charity and parish life."[154]

The pope reminded us that Christ was "the first deacon," and in his letter to the Galatians, St. Paul describes himself as an "apostle" and a "servant." "They are like the two sides of a medal," the Holy Father added, because "those who proclaim Jesus are called to serve, and those who serve proclaim Jesus." Therefore,

---

154 Pope Francis, Homily at Mass for the Jubilee of Deacons (May 29, 2016).

"a disciple of Jesus cannot take a road other than that of the Master. If he wants to proclaim him, he must imitate him. Like Paul, he must strive to become a servant." Indeed, "if evangelizing is the mission entrusted at baptism to each Christian, serving is the way that mission is carried out. It is the only way to be a disciple of Jesus. His witnesses are those who do as he did: those who serve their brothers and sisters, never tiring of following Christ in his humility, never wearing of the Christian life, which is a life of service."

Pope Francis continued, "One who serves cannot hoard his free time," but "he has to give up the idea of being the master of his day." He is not "a slave to his own agenda," but "ever ready to deal with the unexpected," "ever available," "ever open to God's constant surprises," "not self-serving." Therefore, he knows how to open "the doors of his time and inner space for those around him, including those who knock on those doors at odd hours, even if that entails setting aside something he likes to do or giving up some well-deserved rest."

The Gospel passage on the day of the Jubilee of Deacons tells the story of the centurion who, not wanting to disturb the Master, implores Jesus with extreme delicately to cure his servant. "Jesus marvels at these words. He is struck by the centurion's great humility, by his meekness. And meekness is one of the virtues of deacons." "Given his troubles, the centurion might have been anxious and could have demanded to be heard, making his authority felt. He could have insisted and even forced Jesus to come to his house. Instead, he was modest, unassuming and meek; he did not raise his voice or make a fuss. He acted, perhaps without even being aware of it, like God himself, who is meek and humble of heart." These are also the "characteristics of Christian service; meek and humble, it imitates God by serving others: by welcoming them with patient love and unflagging sympathy, by making them feel welcome and at home in the ecclesial community, where the greatest are not those who command but those who serve." And—the pope adds—"never shout, never!"

It is, therefore, a mission that, by its very nature, involves all Christians, who are called to bear witness to the Gospel in this new millennium characterized by divisions and contradictions before which the proclamation of the Kingdom must resound as a *prophecy* and at the same time, a *concrete commitment*.

While engaging in the world is a possible and the right and proper field of action for the laity, the matter is more complex for deacons, who are called to be a visible sign of the *diaconia* of Christ and the Church both in the Christian community and in society. They are called to be a sign of Christ's love, especially for the poor and the needy. Indeed, deacons are constantly called to care for the *meaning* of man's existence, in whatever condition he finds himself.

With these observations, the pope invites us to reinterpret the vast world of parish territories as *relationship workshops* in order to reiterate the centrality of man—who realizes his identity as a person through his relationship with others—and the Church's role throughout history as *an expert in humanity*. This premise allows us to identify some main areas of pastoral work that can serve as experiments or laboratories in communities for the care of relationships and collaboration. In this context, the service of the deacon can make a valuable contribution toward fostering pastoral action that is characterized by concreteness of immediate interpersonal relationships that will allow for the "sharing" of every joy and every pain. Like every member of the People of God, deacons live and fulfill their mission according to the concrete historical context in which their ministry is carried out; and this pastoral approach that is carried out in neighborhoods and residential areas, in families, and in the areas farthest from the parish, leads to the gradual organizational transformation of the community, giving greater value to its different components and each person's contribution to the common good, according to the gifts he has received from the Spirit.

# The Words of Pope Francis

## Angelus

*Dear Brothers and Sisters! Good morning!*

First of all I would like to share with you the joy of having met, yesterday and today, a special pilgrimage for the Year of Faith of seminarians and novices. I ask you to pray for them, that love of Christ may always grow in their lives and that they may become true missionaries of the Kingdom of God.

The Gospel this Sunday (Lk 10:1-12, 17-20) speaks to us about this: the fact that Jesus is not a lone missionary, he does not want to fulfill his mission alone, but involves his disciples. And today we see that in addition to the twelve Apostles he calls another seventy-two, and sends them to the villages, two by two, to proclaim that the Kingdom of God is close at hand. This is very beautiful! Jesus does not want to act alone, he came to bring the love of God into the world and he wants to spread it in the style of communion, in the style of brotherhood. That is why he immediately forms a community of disciples, which is a missionary community. He trains them straight away for the mission, to go forth.

But pay attention: their purpose is not to socialize, to spend time together, no, their purpose is to proclaim the Kingdom of God, and this is urgent! And it is still urgent today! There is no time to be lost in gossip, there is no need to wait for everyone's consensus, what is necessary is to go out and proclaim. To all people you bring the peace of Christ, and if they do not welcome it, you go ahead just the same. To the sick you bring healing, because God wants to heal man of every evil. How many missionaries do this, they sow life, health, comfort to the outskirts of the world. How beautiful it is! Do not live for yourselves, do not live for yourselves, but live to go forth and do good! There are many young people today in the Square: think of this, ask yourselves this: is Jesus calling me to go forth, to come out of myself to do good? To you, young people, to you boys and girls I ask: you, are you brave enough for this, do you have the courage to hear the voice of Jesus? It is beautiful to be missionaries! . . . Ah, you are good! I like this!

These seventy-two disciples, whom Jesus sent out ahead of him, who were they? Who do they represent? If the Twelve were the Apostles, and also thus represent the Bishops, their successors, these seventy-two could represent the other ordained ministries, priests and deacons; but more broadly we can think of the other ministries in the Church, of catechists, of the lay faithful who engage in parish missions, of those who work with the sick, with different kinds of disadvantaged and marginalized people; but always as missionaries of the Gospel, with the urgency of the Kingdom that is close at hand.

Everyone must be a missionary, everyone can hear that call of Jesus and go forth and proclaim the Kingdom!

The Gospel says that those seventy-two came back from their mission full of joy, because they had experienced the power of Christ's Name over evil. Jesus says it: to these disciples He gives the power to defeat the evil one. But he adds: "Do not rejoice in this, that the spirits are subject to you; but rejoice that your names are written in heaven" (Lk 10:20). We should not boast as if we were the protagonists: there is only one protagonist, it is the Lord! The Lord's grace is the protagonist! He is the one hero! And our joy is just this: to be his disciples, his friends. May Our Lady help us to be good agents of the Gospel.

Dear friends, be glad! Do not be afraid of being joyful! Don't be afraid of joy! That joy which the Lord gives us when we allow him to enter our life. Let us allow him to enter our lives and invite us to go out to the margins of life and proclaim the Gospel. Don't be afraid of joy. Have joy and courage!

Sunday, July 7, 2013

# Homily for the Extraordinary Jubilee of Deacons

"A servant of Jesus Christ" (Gal 1:10). We have listened to these words that the Apostle Paul, writing to the Galatians, uses to describe himself. At the beginning of his Letter, he had presented himself as "an apostle" by the will of the Lord Jesus (cf. Gal 1:1). These two terms—apostle and servant—go together. They can never be separated. They are like the two sides of a medal. Those who proclaim Jesus are called to serve, and those who serve proclaim Jesus.

The Lord was the first to show us this. He, the Word of the Father, who brought us the good news (Is 61:1), indeed, who is the good news (cf. Lk 4:18), became our servant (Phil 2:7). He came "not to be served, but to serve" (Mk 10:45). "He became the servant (*diakonos*) of all," wrote one of the Church Fathers (St. Polycarp, *Ad Phil.* V, 2). We who proclaim him are called to act as he did, "merciful, zealous, walking according to the charity of the Lord who made himself the servant of all" (*ibid.*). A disciple of Jesus cannot take a road other than that of the Master. If he wants to proclaim him, he must imitate him. Like Paul, he must *strive to become a servant.* In other words, if *evangelizing* is the mission entrusted at baptism to each Christian, *serving* is the way that mission is carried out. It is the only way to be a disciple of Jesus. His witnesses are those who do as he did: those who serve their brothers and sisters, never tiring of following Christ in his humility, never wearing of the Christian life, which is *a life of service.*

How do we become "good and faithful servants" (cf. Mt 25:21)? As a first step, we are asked to be *available.* A servant daily learns detachment from doing everything his own way and living his life as he would. Each morning he trains himself to be generous with his life and to realize that the rest of the day will not be his own, but given over to others. One who serves cannot hoard his free time; he has to give up the idea of being the master of his day. He knows that his time is not his own, but a gift from God which is then offered back to him. Only in this way will it bear fruit. One who serves is not a slave to his own agenda, but ever ready to deal with the unexpected, ever available to his brothers and sisters and ever open to God's constant surprises. One who serves is open to surprises, to God's constant surprises. A servant knows how to open the doors of his time and inner space for those around him, including those who knock on those doors at odd hours, even if that entails setting aside something he likes to do or giving up some well-deserved rest. One who serves is not worried about the timetable. It deeply troubles me when I see a timetable in a parish: "From such a time to such a time." And then? There is no open door, no priest, no deacon, no layperson to receive people. . . . This is not good. Don't worry about the timetable: have the courage to look past the timetable. In this way, dear deacons, if you show that you are available to others, your ministry will not be self-serving, but evangelically fruitful.

Today's Gospel also speaks to us of service. It shows us two servants who have much to teach us: the servant of the centurion whom Jesus cures and the centurion himself, who serves the Emperor. The words used by the centurion to dissuade Jesus from coming to his house are remarkable, and often the very opposite of our own: "Lord, do not trouble yourself, for I am not worthy to have you come under my roof" (Lk 7:6); "I did not presume to come to you" (7:7); "I also am a man set under authority" (7:8). Jesus marvels at these words. He is struck by the centurion's great humility, by his *meekness*. And meekness is one of the virtues of deacons. When a deacon is meek, then he is one who serves, who is not trying to "mimic" priests; no, he is meek. Given his troubles, the centurion might have been anxious and could have demanded to be heard, making his authority felt. He could have insisted and even forced Jesus to come to his house. Instead, he was modest, unassuming and meek; he did not raise his voice or make a fuss. He acted, perhaps without even being aware of it, like God himself, who is "meek and humble of heart" (Mt 11:29). For God, who is love, out of love is ever ready to serve us. He is patient, kind and always there for us; he suffers for our mistakes and seeks the way to help us improve. These are the characteristics of Christian service; meek and humble, it *imitates God by serving others*: by welcoming them with patient love and unflagging sympathy, by making them feel welcome and at home in the ecclesial community, where the greatest are not those who command but those who serve (cf. Lk 22:26). And never shout, never. This, dear deacons, is how your vocation as ministers of charity will mature: in meekness.

After the Apostle Paul and the centurion, today's readings show us a third servant, the one whom Jesus heals. The Gospel tells us that he was dear to his master and was sick, without naming his grave illness (v. 2). In a certain sense, we can see ourselves in that servant. Each of us is very dear to God, who loves us, chooses us and calls us to serve. Yet each of us needs first to be healed inwardly. To be ready to serve, we need a healthy heart: a heart healed by God, one which knows forgiveness and is neither closed nor hardened. We would do well each day to pray trustingly for this, asking to be healed by Jesus, to grow more like him who "no longer calls us servants but friends" (cf. Jn 15:15). Dear deacons, this is a grace you can implore daily in prayer. You can offer the Lord your work, your little inconveniences, your weariness and your hopes in an authentic prayer that brings your life to the Lord and the Lord to your life. When you serve at the table of the Eucharist, there you will find the presence of Jesus, who gives himself to you so that you can give yourselves to others.

In this way, available in life, meek of heart and in constant dialogue with Jesus, you will not be afraid to be *servants of Christ*, and to encounter and caress the flesh of the Lord in the poor of our time.

Sunday, May 29, 2016

## Angelus

At the end of this celebration, I wish to extend a special greeting to you, dear deacons, who have come from Italy and other countries. Thanks for your presence here today, but most of all, your presence in the Church! . . . For these intentions, let us invoke the intercession of the Virgin Mary, as we entrust to her the life and ministry of all the deacons in the world.

Sunday, May 29, 2016

# PART IX

# The Diaconate and the Vocation to Martyrdom

Martyrdom, from the Greek word *màrtys*, meaning "witness," the one who proclaims, attests to, and shouts the joy of the Resurrection. He is the one who announces the victory of life over death, of love over hate, of justice over abuse. On the great morning of his martyrdom, it was Stephen, the humble deacon from the Acts of the Apostles, who Luke entrusted with the "crown" (*stèfanos*) of witness.

Stephen was Jewish by birth. He is venerated as a saint by the Catholic Church and the Orthodox Church. "The story of his martyrdom comes to us from the Acts of the Apostles, where we can read about his call to service (to the diaconia of the disciples), as well as his martyrdom by stoning in the presence of Paul (Saul of Tarsus) before his conversion."[155]

"The date of Stephen's death can be determined with a certain degree of certainty because of how it happened. The fact that he was not killed by crucifixion

---

155 "Stephan Protomartyr," ("*Stefano protomartire*"), *Wikipedia Italia*, *https://it.wikipedia.org/wiki/Stefano_protomartire* (accessed March 26, 2018).

(the method used by the occupying Romans), but by stoning, means that his death occurred during the administrative vacuum that followed the removal of Pontius Pilate (AD 36), who had become an enemy of the people due to the excessive violence he used to sedate the so-called Samaritan revolt at Mount Gerizim. Thus, Palestine was being governed by the Sanhedrin at the time, who executed the death sentence through stoning, in accordance with local tradition. In the Acts of the Apostles, it is written that Stephen became an enemy of some freedmen, who probably received that name for being descendants of Jewish people who had been enslaved by Pompey (69 BC) and then freed."[156]

"'Lord, do not hold this sin against them,' he prayed for his killers (Acts 7:60), a scandalous echo of Jesus' own voice, in his last breath. In a speech that is representative of all biblical history, Stephen narrates God's sodality with the world throughout a time of caring and Love that started in the beginning, was present with Jesus Christ, and that continues to grow to this day."[157]

---

156 "Stephan Protomartyr," ("*Stefano protomartire*"), *Wikipedia Italia*.

157 Rosanna Virgili, "The Foundational Values of a Community to Be Rebuilt. Christian Martyrdom, Not a Sacrifice But a Happy Message," ("*I valori fondanti di una comunità da ricostruire. Il martirio cristiano, non sacrificio ma lieto messaggio*"), *Avvenire.it*, July 30, 2016, originally published in Italian: *https://www.avvenire.it/opinioni/pagine/martiri-e-figli-quale-signifcato-nel-vuoto-di-identit-europeo-* (accessed May 2, 2018).

"For his valuable witness, Stephen earned the title of 'protomartyr' of the Church, becoming a true pillar of the Church. He bore witness with such strength and passion that he was hated by many who 'crowned' him with the blows of stones and with blood. Martyrdom, therefore, is the outpouring of Gospel proclamation; it is the splendor of a Word that is Good News for the poor, the oppressed, and the imprisoned, which no one can extinguish, not even with disfigurement, torture, or contempt."[158]

It is tradition for the pope to celebrate the *Angelus* every year on December 26 for the Feast of St. Stephen. "And on this second day of the octave," Pope Francis says, "the Feast of St. Stephen, the first martyr of the Church, is inserted into the joy of Christmas. The book of the Acts of the Apostles presents him to us as 'a man full of faith and of the Holy Spirit' (6:5), chosen with six others for the service of widows and the poor in the first Community of Jerusalem. And it tells us about his martyrdom, when after a fiery dispute that aroused the anger of the members of the Sanhedrin, he was dragged outside the city walls and stoned. Stephen dies like Jesus, asking pardon for those who killed him (7:55-60)."[159] On the day of Stephen's martyrdom, where the Church sees in the sacrifice of

---

158 Rosanna Virgili, "The Foundational Values."

159 Pope Francis, *Angelus* (December 26, 2013).

martyrs their "birth into heaven," Francis warns us against looking at the birth of Jesus as a fairytale for children, so that "the remembrance of the first martyr immediately dispels a false image of Christmas," an image that is "the fairytale, sugarcoated image, which is not in the Gospel!"

It is interesting to note, and it is no coincidence, that the first martyr is, in fact, a deacon. It is often forgotten that Stephen is the Christian deacon protomartyr, that is, the first to have given his life to bear witness to his faith in Christ and to spread the Gospel. Stephen was the first of the seven deacons chosen by the Apostles to help them in the ministry of the faith.

Having created a way of life dictated by a faith that did not conform to religious traditions and having been accused by everyone of attracting the fury of betrayed gods, the deacons were the first to suffer the pressure and persecution of the ancient city, which was hostile toward their message and their way of life. We find proof of this in stories of persecution where deacons are present alongside martyrs. One example is the diary of Perpetua, one of the most famous figures in the martyrology of Carthage at the beginning of the third century.[160]

Traditionally, the institution of the "seven" (Acts 6:1-7) to "serve at table" (*diakonéin trapézais*) instead of the Apostles, who reserved for themselves the tasks of

---

160 "After a few days we are taken into the dungeon, and I was very much afraid, because I had never felt such darkness. O terrible day! O the fierce heat of the shock of the soldiery, because of the crowds! I was very unusually distressed by my anxiety for my infant. There were present there Tertius and Pomponius, the blessed deacons who ministered to us, and had arranged by means of a gratuity that we might be refreshed by being sent out for a few hours into a pleasanter part of the prison. Then going out of the dungeon, all attended to their own wants. I suckled my child, which was now enfeebled with hunger. . . . Such solicitude I suffered for many days, and I obtained for my infant to remain in the dungeon with me; and forthwith I grew strong and was relieved from distress and anxiety about my infant. . . .

"The procurator then delivers judgment on all of us, and condemns us to the wild beasts, and we went down cheerfully to the dungeon. Then, because my child had been used to receive suck from me, and to stay with me in the prison, I send Pomponius the deacon to my father to ask for the infant, but my father would not give it [to] him.

"The day before that on which we were to fight, I saw in a vision that Pomponius the deacon came hither to the gate of the prison, and knocked vehemently. I went out to him, and opened the gate for him; and he was clothed in a richly ornamented white robe, and he had on manifold calliculæ. And he said to me, 'Perpetua, we are waiting for you; come!' And he held his hand to me, and we began to go through rough and winding places. Scarcely at length had we arrived breathless at the amphitheater, when he led me into the middle of the arena, and said to me, 'Do not fear, I am here with you, and I am laboring with you;' and he departed."

("The Passion of the Holy Martyrs Perpetua and Felicitas," Rev R. E. Wallis, PhD, translator, in *Ante-Nicene Fathers*, Volume 3: Tertullian, Part 3: Ethical (Grand Rapids, Michigan: WM. B. Eerdmans Publishing Company) 700-703, *http://www.ccel.org/ccel/schaff/anf03.vi.vi.ii.html#fnf_vi.vi.ii-p3.2* [accessed May 15, 2018].)

"prayer" and "ministry of the word," is considered to be the institution of the "diaconate" in the Church. The Liturgy even references this passage from Acts on the occasion of the conferral of the diaconal order.

It should also be noted that the actions carried out by at least two of the "seven," namely Stephen and Philip, far exceed the initial purpose for which the "seven" were instituted: they act more like preachers and representatives of the group than ministers of charity. They are more similar to Apostles, even though they are their subordinates, than to actual deacons.

Stephen is portrayed, above all else, as a great preacher and polemicist, full of *grace* and the "Holy Spirit" (Acts 7:8-55), an agent of "wonders" and "signs" (Acts 6-8), in the likeness of the Apostles. Stephen's solemn and lengthy speech, the longest one in the Acts of the Apostles (7:2-53), shows us, not only his knowledge of Scripture, but more importantly, his ability to interpret it in light of the Christ event: in some ways, he is a precursor to Paul!

Precisely for this reason, the pope affirms that "following the Gospel is certainly a demanding but beautiful, very beautiful journey, and those who follow it with faithfulness and courage receive the reward promised by the Lord to men and women of good will. As the angels sang on Christmas Day: 'Peace! Peace!'" This peace granted by God is capable of calming the conscience of those who, through the trials of life, are able to receive the Word of God and commit themselves to observing it with perseverance to the end (cf. Mt 10:22)."[161]

And the deacon accepted the Word of God as a priority commitment on the day of ordination. The bishop says: "Receive the Gospel of Christ, whose herald you now are. Believe what you read, teach what you believe and practice what you teach." How does diaconal service fit into the ecclesial service to the Word of God?

I think it is important to point out a "liturgical icon" so that the icon that is the Liturgy is and remains the "source and summit" of the entire life of the Church. At the center of liturgical action is the Holy Altar, where we find the Holy Gospel and the Divine Eucharist through which the Wisdom Word Incarnate gives us the Spirit who glorifies us. The deacon takes the Gospel of grace and mercy from the altar, where it rests permanently, and carries it with regal solemnity to the ambo, where it will be proclaimed by the deacon himself, mystagogically explained by the bishop or priest, and listened to by the faithful. Thus, from the diaconia of the Word comes a true ministry of the Word, which finds its biblical source and its specific ecclesial identity in evangelizing the last and the marginalized. In fact, the deacon is "*teacher* insofar as he preaches and bears witness the Word of God; he *sanctifies* when he administers the Sacrament of Baptism, the Holy Eucharist and the

---

161 Pope Francis, *Angelus* (December 26, 2014).

Sacramentals; . . . he is a *guide* inasmuch as he animates the community or a section of ecclesial life."[162] Like the priestly order, diaconal service is made up of teaching, sanctifying, and guiding. This is why it is fundamental to the ordained diaconia to recognize the deacon's concrete aptitude to be the animator of the service of the Word, not only of the Liturgy and charity, in the community to which he belongs. Regarding the diaconia of the Word, once again, it is the *presentation of the Gospel Book* during the Ordination of the deacon that shows us the clear link between the place that the new deacon will occupy in the Church and the way to exercise his ministry. Proclaim the Gospel and practice what it teaches: it is in these dynamic terms that the Church entrusts the newly ordained with the *diaconia* of the Word. Only prolonged and varied practice will reveal the deep meaning of a word proclaimed by a person who is sacramentally ordained but who, nevertheless, is not removed from his family, his cultural environment, or his profane work. The condition of being ordained is a new reality for today's Church. The restoration of the permanent diaconate can help reconstruct the fabric of the Church so that the vision of Vatican II, which sees the People of God as the fundamental ecclesial reality, can be lived in its broadest sense. It is here that we discover the importance of the fact that the deacon is *a word in*

---

162 *Directory*, no. 22.

*action*, not only on a moral level, but on a sacramental level: the more his life represents a faithful expression of the Word that he proclaims, the more he becomes a sign of the efficacy of this Word, which is always alive in the hearts of men. Therefore, it is not the mere presence of the deacon in man's daily life that guarantees the efficacy of the Word, but the opposite. It is when the deacon fortifies himself in and of the Word that his presence becomes an effective sign, a sign capable of evoking One who is greater than he.

Indeed, it is the introduction of the deacon into the apostolic ministry that makes this meaning possible. By exercising a ministry proper to the episcopate, namely evangelical preaching, the deacon makes present an ecclesial reality of utmost importance: the bishop, in the Word that he preaches by virtue of his role, is at the service of the Body of Christ. And since the deacon's preaching of the Word must lead back to the diaconal character of episcopal preaching, the deacon will avoid anything that might distance himself from the people he is ordained to serve. Today, as we said above, the deacon's job is one of bringing together: not only does he make the Word he proclaims more credible, but he also brings those most responsible for the Word—the bishops—closer to the People of God, making it clear that episcopal preaching is at the service of the Gospel for all men.

The concrete ways in which the deacon exercises the ministry of the Word pass through the main way of *lectio divina* precisely to reiterate the primacy of the Word itself, which is presented as an ordinary place and a real occasion for diaconal "ministeriality." Gospel proclamation requires deacons to have a sincere and faithful love of the Word but also to engage in effective evangelizing work. This work can be realized in different forms, but it cannot be reduced to just the liturgical proclamation of the Gospel, because "following the Gospel is certainly a demanding but beautiful, very beautiful journey, and those who follow it with faithfulness and courage receive the reward promised by the Lord to men and women of good will. As the angels sang on Christmas Day: 'Peace! Peace!'"[163] The "diaconia of peace" that deacons must embody in their service for the Church and for the world is characterized and expressed as the diaconia of *faith*, the diaconia of *hope*, and the diaconia of *charity*. The *diaconia of faith* appears perfectly in the deacon Stephen, who bears witness before those who sit in judgement against him by reading the history of Israel as a story of God's faithful love for his people. Faithful to the point of martyrdom, he shows us that Jesus is "the true Emmanuel," the One who is always "with" us and, at the same time, "beyond" us, beyond every success and triumph, beyond every defeat and victory. He is the

---

163 *Angelus* (December 26, 2014).

future that we must walk toward, knowing in our hearts that he will remain eternally true to his promises.

This makes us understand, the pope affirms, "that in the trials accepted as the result of faith, violence is conquered by love, death by life. And to truly welcome Jesus into our life and to prolong the joy of the Holy Night, the path is the very one indicated by this Gospel, that is, to bear witness to Jesus in humility, in silent service, without fear of going against the current and of paying in the first person."[164] The best-known example of humility is certainly Francis of Assisi, whose name the pope took as Bishop of Rome. It is well known that the diaconia of charity played an important role in Francis's life; he was the deacon par excellence, and in every sick person—particularly in lepers—he saw the incarnation of the suffering and crucified Christ. Like in *Poverello*, the poor man generally reacquires the theological meaning that the Christ of the Gospels gave to him, that of being the privileged recipient of divine mercy: "Let all the brothers strive to follow the humility and poverty of our Lord Jesus Christ. . . . [He] was poor, and a stranger, and lived on alms, He Himself and the Blessed Virgin and His disciples. . . . And alms is an inheritance and a right which is due to the poor, which our Lord Jesus Christ purchased for us. And the brothers who labor in seeking it will have a great recompense, and they will

---

164 *Angelus* (December 26, 2014).

procure and acquire a reward for those who give; for all that men leave in this world shall perish, but for the charity and alms deeds they have done they will receive a reward from God."[165]

"And if not all are called, like St. Stephen, to shed their blood, each Christian is, however, asked to be consistent in every circumstance with the faith that he or she professes. And Christian consistency is a grace that we must ask of the Lord. To be consistent, to live as Christians and not to say: 'I am a Christian,' but live as a pagan. Consistency is a grace we must ask for today."[166] It is for this reason that deacons must accept the way of martyrdom, "which continues to be present in the history of the Church, from Stephen up to our time,"[167] as the spiritual source in their lives.

Then again, the fact that Stephen is mainly targeted by fanatical Hellenists signifies not only the influence that he must have exercised over the people—to the point of creating a sort of public danger—but also his authority within the Church: once he was eliminated, everything could go back to normal! And so, "in the martyrdom of Stephen, [we see] the same confrontation between good and evil, between hatred and forgiveness, between meekness and violence, which culminated in

---

165  Excerpts from the first rule of Francis of Assisi.

166  *Angelus* (December 26, 2014).

167  Pope Francis, *Angelus* (December 26, 2016).

the Cross of Christ."[168] Each Christian is born of God's forgiveness. Using the example of Stephen, Francis tells us that there is a special element in the Acts of the Apostles that draws the deacon closer to the Lord. "It is his *forgiveness before* he is stoned to *death*. Nailed to the cross, Jesus said, 'Father, forgive them; for they know not what they do' (Lk 23:34). Likewise, Stephen 'knelt down and cried with a loud voice, "Lord, do not hold this sin against them"' (Acts 7:60). Stephen is therefore a *martyr, which means witness, because he does as Jesus did*. Indeed, true witnesses are those who act as He did: those who pray, who love, who give, but above all those who *forgive*, because forgiveness, as the word itself says, is the highest expression of giving. We could ask, however, what good is it to forgive? Is it merely a good deed or does it bring results? We find an answer in the very martyrdom of Stephen. Among those for whom he implores forgiveness there is a young man named Saul; this man persecuted the Church and tried to destroy her (cf. Acts 8:3). Shortly thereafter Saul becomes Paul, the great saint, the apostle of the people. He has received Stephen's forgiveness. We could say that Paul is born by the grace of God and by Stephen's forgiveness."[169] This is a truly important step for the diaconal ministry, to teach forgiveness and reconciliation through mercy.

168 *Angelus* (December 26, 2013).

169 *Angelus* (December 26, 2016).

For this reason, Francis invites us to recover our spiritual convictions, in the strength of faith in the Father of mercy. He invites us to recover the strength of merciful love. It took courage to say this, and we have to be just as courageous to put it into practice. Many people today are confused between condescending pity, contempt, and hate, and are thirsty for true tenderness, tenderness that is the reflection and promise of God's tenderness. In the *Angelus* from December 26, 2015, we are called to reflect on how "yesterday we contemplated the merciful love of God, who became flesh for us. Today we see the consistent response of Jesus' disciple, who gives his life. Yesterday the Savior was born on earth; today his faithful servant is born in heaven. Yesterday, as today, the shadows of the rejection of life appear, but the light of love—which conquers hatred and inaugurates a new world—shines even brighter." This new world evokes the Beatitude that summarizes the entire life and teachings of Jesus perfectly: Blessed are the merciful, for they will be shown mercy.

Pope Francis cites Luke in the Bull of Indiction of the Extraordinary Jubilee of Mercy, *Misericordiae Vultus*: "Be merciful just as your Father is merciful" (Lk 6:36). This call echoes Matthew's maxim: "So be perfect, just as your heavenly Father is perfect" (Mt 5:48). "Blessed are the merciful," according to Pope Francis, does not mean finding a moment to be good and to make a gesture of mercy. It is only when we make a habit out of doing good and helping others that we find mercy. God sees himself in the oppressed, in history's victims, and he shares in the suffering of the poor and needy. "The apostle James"—the pope writes—"teaches that our mercy to others will vindicate us on the day of God's judgment. . . . Mercy triumphs over judgment (Jas 2:12-13). Here James is faithful to the finest tradition of post-exilic Jewish spirituality, which attributed a particular salutary value to mercy."[170] This shows the urgency to assume a behavior that is rooted in the Beatitudes and that, through the behavior of Christ's disciples, restores the face of Christ himself, Christ who is meek and humble of heart. The true face of God, face that is gift and forgiveness, is at play. Also at play, consequently, is the true face of man.

"Today," the pope concludes the *Angelus* from December 26, 2014, "the Liturgy recalls the witness of St. Stephen, who [was] chosen by the Apostles, along with six others, to carry out the deaconry of charity, that is, to attend to the poor, the orphans, the widows in the community of Jerusalem." In the Office of Readings on the feast of the Holy Deacon, the Liturgy, the teacher of life, shows us *the armor of love*:

> Yesterday we celebrated the birth in time of our eternal King. Today we celebrate the triumphant suffering of his soldier. Yesterday our king, clothed

---

170 EG, no. 193.

in his robe of flesh, left his place in the virgin's womb and graciously visited the world. Today his soldier leaves the tabernacle of his body and goes triumphantly to heaven. Our king, despite his exalted majesty, came in humility for our sake; yet he did not come empty-handed. He brought his soldiers a great gift that not only enriched them but also made them unconquerable in battle, for it was the gift of love, which was to bring men to share in his divinity. He gave of his bounty, yet without any loss to himself. In a marvelous way he changed into wealth the poverty of his faithful followers while remaining in full possession of his own inexhaustible riches. And so the love that brought Christ from heaven to earth raised Stephen from earth to heaven; shown first in the king, it later shone forth in his soldier. Love was Stephen's weapon by which he gained every battle, and so won the crown signified by his name. His love of God kept him from yielding to the ferocious mob; his love for his neighbor made him pray for those who were stoning him. Love inspired him to reprove those who erred, to make them amend; love led him to pray for those who stoned him, to save them from punishment. Strengthened by the power of his love, he overcame the raging cruelty of Saul and won his persecutor on earth as his companion in heaven. In his holy and tireless love he longed to gain by prayer those whom he could not convert by admonition.

Now at last, Paul rejoices with Stephen, with Stephen he delights in the glory of Christ, with Stephen he exalts, with Stephen he reigns. Stephen went first, slain by the stones thrown by Paul, but Paul followed after, helped by the prayer of Stephen. This, surely, is the true life, my brothers, a life in which Paul feels no shame because of Stephen's death, and Stephen delights in Paul's companionship, for love fills them both with joy. It was Stephen's love that prevailed over the cruelty of the mob, and it was Paul's love that covered the multitude of his sins; it was love that won for both of them the kingdom of heaven. Love, indeed, is the source of all good things; it is an impregnable defense, and the way that leads to heaven. He who walks in love can neither go astray nor be afraid: love guides him, protects him, and brings him to his journey's end. My brothers, Christ made love the stairway that would enable all Christians to climb to heaven. Hold fast to it, therefore, in all sincerity, give one another practical proof of it, and by your progress in it, make your ascent together.[171]

This is the path that Jesus indicated to his disciples, as the Gospel attests: "You will be hated by all because

---

171 From a sermon by St. Fulgentius of Ruspe, bishop (*Sermo* 3,1-3,5-6: CCL 91A, 905-909), Liturgy of the Hours, vol. I, Office of Readings, Second Reading, p. 1256.

of my name; but whoever endures to the end will be saved" (Mt 10:22). This is the path that deacons will have to take; they must "[commit] themselves in favor of the least, of the most neglected, doing good to all without distinction; in this way they witness to charity in truth."[172]

172 *Angelus* (December 26, 2016).

# The Words of Pope Francis

## Angelus, Feast of Saint Stephen, Protomartyr

*Dear Brothers and Sisters, Good morning.*

You aren't afraid of the rain, you are very good!

The liturgy extends the Solemnity of Christmas for eight days: a time of joy for the entire People of God! And on this second day of the octave, the Feast of St. Stephen, the first martyr of the Church, is inserted into the joy of Christmas. The book of the Acts of the Apostles presents him to us as "a man full of faith and of the Holy Spirit" (6:5), chosen with six others for the service of widows and the poor in the first Community of Jerusalem. And it tells us about his martyrdom, when after a fiery dispute that aroused the anger of the members of the Sanhedrin, he was dragged outside the city walls and stoned. Stephen dies like Jesus, asking pardon for those who killed him (7:55-60).

In the joyful atmosphere of Christmas, this commemoration may seem out of place. For Christmas is the celebration of life and it fills us with sentiments of serenity and peace. Why disturb the charm with the memory of such atrocious violence? In reality, from the perspective of faith, the Feast of St. Stephen is in full harmony with the deeper meaning of Christmas. In martyrdom, in fact, violence is conquered by love, death by life. The Church sees in the sacrifice of the martyrs their "birth into heaven." Therefore, today we celebrate the "birth" of Stephen, which in its depths springs from the Birth of Christ. Jesus transforms the death of those who love him into a dawn of new life!

In the martyrdom of Stephen the same confrontation between good and evil, between hatred and forgiveness, between meekness and violence, which culminated in the Cross of Christ. Thus, the remembrance of the first martyr immediately dispels a false image of Christmas: the fairytale, sugarcoated image, which is not in the Gospel! The liturgy brings us back to the authentic meaning of the Incarnation, by linking Bethlehem to Calvary and by reminding us that the divine salvation involved the battle against sin, it passes through the narrow door of the Cross. This is the path which Jesus clearly indicated to his disciples, as today's Gospel attests: "You will be hated by all for my name's sake. But he who endures to the end will be saved" (Mt 10:22).

Therefore today we pray especially for the Christians who are discriminated against on account of the witness they bear to Christ and to the Gospel. Let us remain close to these brothers and sisters who, like St. Stephen, are unjustly accused and made the objects of various kinds of violence. Unfortunately, I am sure they are more numerous today than in the early days of the Church. There are so many! This occurs especially where religious freedom is still not guaranteed or fully realized. However, it also happens in countries and areas where on paper freedom and human rights are protected, but where in fact believers, and especially Christians, face restrictions and discrimination. I would like to ask you to take a moment in silence to pray for these brothers and sisters . . . and let us entrust them to Our Lady (Hail Mary . . . ). This comes as no surprise to a Christian, for Jesus foretold it as a propitious occasion to bear witness. Still, on a civil level, injustice must be denounced and eliminated.

May Mary Queen of Martyrs help us to live Christmas with the ardor of faith and love which shone forth in St. Stephen and in all of the martyrs of the Church.

December 26, 2013

*Dear Brothers and Sisters, Good morning,*

Today the Liturgy recalls the witness of St. Stephen, who, chosen by the Apostles, along with six others, to carry out the deaconry of charity, that is, to attend to the poor, the orphans, the widows in the community of Jerusalem, became the first martyr of the Church. Stephen, through his martyrdom, honors the coming of the King of Kings into the world, he bears witness to Him and offers up his very life, as he did in his service to the most needy. And he thereby shows us how to live the mystery of Christmas in its fullness.

The Gospel on this feast day recounts part of Jesus' discourse to his disciples at the time that He sends them on mission. He says, among other things: "You will be hated by all for my name's sake. But he who endures to the end will be saved" (Mt 10:22). These words of the Lord do not disturb the celebration of Christmas, but remove that artificial sugary coating which does not appertain to it. They enable us to understand that in the trials accepted as the result of faith, violence is conquered by love, death by life. And to truly welcome Jesus into our life and to prolong the joy of the Holy Night, the path is the very one indicated by this Gospel, that is, to bear witness to Jesus in humility, in silent service, without fear of going against the current and of paying in the first person. And if not all are called, like St. Stephen, to shed their blood, each Christian is, however, asked to be consistent in every circumstance with the faith that he or she professes. And Christian consistency is a grace that we must ask of the Lord. To be consistent, to live as Christians and not to say: "I am a Christian," but live as a pagan. Consistency is a grace we must ask for today.

Following the Gospel is certainly a demanding but beautiful, very beautiful journey, and those who follow it with faithfulness and courage receive the reward promised by the Lord to men and women of good will. As the angels sang on Christmas Day: "Peace! Peace!" This peace granted by God is capable of calming the conscience of those who, through the trials of life, are able to receive the Word of God and commit themselves to observing it with perseverance to the end (cf. Mt 10:22).

Today, brothers and sisters, let us pray in a special way for those who are discriminated against, persecuted and killed for bearing witness to Christ. I would like to say to each one of them: if you bear this cross with love, you have entered into the mystery of Christmas, you are in the heart of Christ and of the Church.

Further, let us pray, also because of the sacrifice of these martyrs of today—there are so many, so very many!—that the commitment to recognize and concretely ensure religious freedom be strengthened, as this freedom is an inalienable right of every human being.

Dear brothers and sisters, I hope that you spend the Christmas season peacefully. May St. Stephen, Deacon and First Martyr, sustain us on our daily journey, which we hope to crown, in the end, with the joyous assembly of Saints in Paradise.

Friday, December 26, 2014

*Dear Brothers and Sisters, Good morning!*

Today we celebrate the Feast of St. Stephen. The remembrance of the first martyr follows immediately after the solemnity of Christmas. Yesterday we contemplated the merciful love of God, who became flesh for us. Today we see the consistent response of Jesus' disciple, who gives his life. Yesterday the Savior was born on earth;

today his faithful servant is born in heaven. Yesterday, as today, the shadows of the rejection of life appear, but the light of love—which conquers hatred and inaugurates a new world—shines even brighter. There is a special aspect in today's account of the Acts of the Apostles, which brings St. Stephen close to the Lord. It is his *forgiveness before* he is stoned to *death*. Nailed to the cross, Jesus said, "Father, forgive them; for they know not what they do" (Lk 23:34). Likewise, Stephen "knelt down and cried with a loud voice, 'Lord, do not hold this sin against them'" (Acts 7:60). Stephen is therefore a *martyr, which means witness, because he does as Jesus did*. Indeed, true witnesses are those who act as He did: those who pray, who love, who give, but above all those who *forgive*, because forgiveness, as the word itself says, is the highest expression of giving.

We could ask, however, what good is it to forgive? Is it merely a good deed or does it bring results? We find an answer in the very martyrdom of Stephen. Among those for whom he implores forgiveness there is a young man named Saul; this man persecuted the Church and tried to destroy her (cf. Acts 8:3). Shortly thereafter Saul becomes Paul, the great saint, the apostle of the people. He has received Stephen's forgiveness. We could say that Paul is born by the grace of God and by Stephen's forgiveness.

We too are *born by the forgiveness of God*. Not only in Baptism, but each time we are forgiven our heart is reborn, it is *renewed*. With each step forward in the life of faith the sign of divine mercy is imprinted anew. For only when we are loved are we in turn able to love. Let us remember this, it will be good for us: if we wish to progress in faith, first of all we must receive God's forgiveness; we must meet the Father, who is willing to forgive all things, always, and who precisely in forgiving heals the heart and rekindles love. We must never tire of asking for divine forgiveness, because only when we are forgiven, when we feel we are forgiven, do we learn to forgive.

Forgiving, however, is not an easy thing, it is always very difficult. How can we imitate Jesus? From what point do we begin to pardon the small and great wrongs that we suffer each day? First of all, *beginning with prayer, as St. Stephen did.* We begin with our own heart: with prayer we are able to face the resentment we feel, by *entrusting to God's mercy those who have wronged us*: "Lord, I ask you for him, I ask you for her." Then we discover that this inner struggle to forgive cleanses us of evil, and that prayer and love free us from the interior chains of bitterness. It is so awful to live in bitterness! Every day we have the opportunity to practice forgiving, to live a gesture so lofty that it brings man closer to God. Like our heavenly Father, may we too become merciful, because through forgiveness, *we conquer evil with good*, we transform hatred into love and in this way we make the world cleaner.

May the Virgin Mary, to whom we entrust those—and unfortunately there are so many—who like St. Stephen suffer persecution in the name of the faith, our many martyrs of today, direct our prayer to receive and give forgiveness. Receive and give forgiveness.

Saturday, December 26, 2015

*Dear Brothers and Sisters, Good morning!*

The joy of Christmas fills our hearts today too, as the liturgy involves us in celebrating the martyrdom of St. Stephen, the First Martyr, inviting us to reflect on the witness that he gave us with his sacrifice. It is precisely the glorious witness of Christian martyrdom, suffered for love of Christ; the martyrdom which continues to be present in the history of the Church, from Stephen up to our time.

Today's Gospel (cf. Mt 10:17-22) told us of this witness. Jesus forewarns the disciples of the rejection and persecution they will encounter: "You will be hated by all for my name's sake" (v. 22). But why does the world persecute Christians? The world hates Christians for the same reason that they hated Jesus: because he brought the light of God, and the world prefers darkness so as to hide its evil works. Let us recall that Jesus himself, at the Last Supper, prayed that the Father might protect us from the wicked worldly spirit. There is opposition between the Gospel and this worldly mentality.

Following Jesus means following his light, which was kindled in the night of Bethlehem, and abandoning worldly obscurity.

The Protomartyr Stephen, full of the Holy Spirit, was stoned because he professed his faith in Jesus Christ, the Son of God. The Only Begotten Son who comes into the world invites every believer to choose the way of light and life. This is the meaning of his coming among us. Loving the Lord and obeying his voice, the Deacon Stephen chose Christ, Life and Light for all mankind. By choosing truth, he became at the same time a victim of the inexplicable iniquity present in the world. But in Christ, Stephen triumphed!

Today too, in order to bear witness to light and to truth, the Church experiences, in different places, harsh persecution, up to the supreme sacrifice of martyrdom. How many of our brothers and sisters in faith endure abuse and violence, and are hated because of Jesus! I shall tell you something: today's martyrs are more numerous with respect to those of the first centuries. When we read the history of the first centuries, here in Rome, we read of so much cruelty toward Christians; I tell you: there is the same cruelty today, and to a greater extent, toward Christians. Today we should think of those who are suffering from persecution, and to be close to them with our affection, our prayers and also our tears. Yesterday, Christmas Day, Christians persecuted in Iraq celebrated

Christmas in their destroyed cathedral: it is an example of faithfulness to the Gospel.

[ . . . ]

Let us raise our prayers to the Virgin Mary, Mother of God and Queen of Martyrs, that she may guide us and always sustain us on our journey in following Jesus Christ, whom we contemplate in the grotto of the Nativity and who is the faithful Witness of God the Father.

Saturday, December 26, 2016

# PART X
# The Deacon as the Custodian of Service

A visit with three families in suburban public housing, a meeting with the Ambrosian clergy at the cathedral in the ecclesial heart of the diocese, and lunch with inmates at San Vittore prison: this is how the first part of Pope Francis's trip to Milan began, with his usual privileged attention for the least.

In the cathedral, Francis spoke with those present and answered questions from a priest, a religious woman, and a deacon.

The deacon is Roberto Crespi, who started his question by pointing out that the diaconate entered into the Milanese clergy in 1990 and that there are currently 143 deacons in the diocese. He then adds,

> It is not a large number but it is a significant number. We are men who live their vocation fully; either in marriage or celibacy, but we also live fully in the world of work and of the professions, and therefore bring the clergy into the world of families and the world of work, we bring all those dimensions of beauty and experience but also hardship and at times suffering. So, we ask you: as permanent deacons, what is our

role in giving form to the face [of the] Church that is humble, that is selfless, that is blessed, that we feel she is in her heart, and of which you often speak to us? Thank you for your attention, and I assure you of our prayer, and that of our wives and families.[173]

Pope Francis responds forcefully: "You are not half priests, half laypeople—this would be to 'functionalize' the diaconate—you are the sacrament of service to God and to others. And from this word 'service' there derives all the development of your work, of your vocation, of your being within the Church. A vocation that, like all vocations is not only individual, but lived within the family and with the family; within the People of God and with the People of God." He jokingly added, "You have a mother-in-law."

Continuing his response to Roberto's question, Francis said, "Within the presbytery, you can be an authoritative voice to show the tension there is between duty and will, the tensions that one lives in family life. And also the blessings one lives within family life. But we must be careful not to see deacons as half priests, half laypeople. At the end, they will end up neither one nor the other. No. Looking at them in this way harms us and harms them."

According to the pope, "This way of considering them takes strength from the charism proper to the

173 Pope Francis, Pastoral Visit to Milan (March 25, 2017).

diaconate in the life of the Church. Likewise, the image of the deacon as a sort of intermediary between the faithful and pastors is inappropriate. The diaconate is a specific vocation, a family vocation that requires service as one of the characteristic gifts of the people of God."

The pope uses a wonderful expression: "The deacon is the custodian of service in the Church." In a homily on the Feast of St. Joseph at the beginning of his papacy, Francis spoke about the act of protecting, of being a custodian, stating that

> the vocation of being a "protector," . . . is not just something involving us Christians alone; it also has a prior dimension which is simply human, involving everyone. It means protecting all creation, the beauty of the created world, as the Book of Genesis tells us and as St. Francis of Assisi showed us. It means respecting each of God's creatures and respecting the environment in which we live. It means protecting people, showing loving concern for each and every person, especially children, the elderly, those in need, who are often the last we think about. It means caring for one another in our families: husbands and wives first protect one another, and then, as parents, they care for their children, and children themselves, in time, protect their parents. It means building sincere friendships in which we protect one another in trust, respect, and goodness. In the end, everything has

been entrusted to our protection, and all of us are responsible for it. Be protectors of God's gifts![174]

This depiction of Joseph as a protector, or custodian, is very interesting. How does Joseph exercise his role of protector? Discreetly, humbly, and silently, but with an unfailing presence and utter fidelity, even when he finds it hard to understand. There are so many things that we as deacons do not understand in our ministry, in our relationships with priests, in our interactions with society, and sometimes, even in our family. As deacons, we are called to protect each person, especially the poorest, to protect ourselves.

I would also like to share what Bergoglio said in his homily at Casa Santa Marta on March 20, 2017. He stated that Joseph is also the guardian of weaknesses. "Indeed, 'Joseph is able to cause many beautiful things to be born out of our weaknesses, out of our sins.' He is the 'guardian of weaknesses so that they may become firm in the faith.' It is a fundamental responsibility which Joseph 'received in a dream' because he was a man who was 'capable of dreaming.' . . . Thus, not only is he 'guardian of our weaknesses, but we can also say that he is the guardian of God's dream: the dream of our Father, the dream of God, of redemption, of saving us

---

174 Pope Francis, Homily at Mass for the Beginning of the Petrine Ministry of the Bishop of Rome (March 19, 2013).

all, of this re-creation entrusted to him."[175] This is Pope Francis's "dream" for the men and women who must witness Christ. It is up to us to put our hearts, hands, and heads into making this "dream" a reality.

Therefore, the pope says our every word must be carefully measured. "You are the guardians of service in the Church: service to the Word, service to the Altar, service to the poor. And your mission, the mission of the deacon, and your contribution consist in this: in reminding us all that faith, in its various expressions— community liturgy, personal prayer, the various forms of charity—and in its various states of life—lay, clerical, family—possesses an essential dimension of service. Service to God and to brothers."[176]

For Francis, therefore, the key to understanding the ministry of deacons is service. Indeed, the pope

[likes] it very much when [in the Acts of the Apostles] the first Hellenistic Christians went to the apostles to complain because their widows and orphans were not well cared for, and they had a meeting, that 'synod' between apostles and disciples, and they 'invented' the deacons to serve. And this is very interesting for us bishops too, because they were all bishops, those who 'made' the deacons. And what does this tell us? That deacons were servants.

175 Pope Francis, Morning Meditation (March 20, 2017).

176 Pastoral Visit (March 25, 2017).

Then they understood that, in that case, it was to assist widows and orphans: but to serve. And to us as bishops: prayer and the proclamation of the Word; and this shows us what the most important charism of a bishop is: to pray. What is the task of a bishop, the first task? Prayer. Second task: proclaiming the Word. But you can see the difference clearly. And for you [deacons]: service.[177]

For Pope Francis, the danger is clericalism, beware of clericalism. And another temptation is functionalism: it is a help that the priest has for this or that; a boy to carry out certain tasks and not for other things. No. You have a clear charism in the Church and you must build it.

"And how far we have to go in this sense! . . . Therein lies the value of the charisms in the Church, which are a memory and a gift for helping all the people of God not to lose the perspective and wealth of God's action." "In summary," the pope concluded,

- there is no altar service, there is no liturgy that is not open to the poor, and; there is no service to the poor that does not lead to the liturgy; and
- there is no ecclesial vocation that is not of the family.

---

177 Pastoral Visit (March 25, 2017).

This helps us to reevaluate the diaconate as an ecclesial vocation. Finally, today it seems that everything must be useful to us, as if everything were targeted at the individual: prayer is useful to me, the community is useful to me, charity is useful to me. You are the gift that the Spirit gives us to show that the right path goes in the opposite direction: in prayer I serve, in the community I serve, with solidarity I serve God and my neighbor.

Let's hope this recommendation on "the value of charisms in the Church, which are a memory and a gift for helping all the people of God not to lose the perspective and wealth of God's action" does not fall on deaf ears.

Vocational co-responsibility is therefore important and is called to express itself through the building of a network among deacons. The goal is to facilitate an *exchange* of innovative and effective "ways of going forth" and the reciprocal communication of experiences in certain areas of service. Making a network also means putting the different paths of ministerial life into communion with one another. Thus, if we want to be deacons in solidarity, we must be able to "build networks": the works of God *are all in collaboration. . . . Let's connect.* This willingness to "build networks" has within it the seed of family closeness. The relational circularity of the family represents the transition from knowing one another to loving care, in line with the principle of love that incorporates all things and that cares for all people. This is even truer for deacons.

*A Church which is poor and for the poor*: this is the wish that has accompanied the ministry of Pope Francis since the beginning; a wish, I might add, that is truly *diaconal*. It is a wish that continually serves as a guiding principle for the spiritual and ecclesial renewal that is outlined so effectively in *Evangelii Gaudium*. Finally, the pope's words to a delegation of the International Diaconate Center on June 4, 2016, can help us reflect: "Deacons manifest the Commandment of Jesus in a particular way: imitating God in the service of others; imitating God who is love and even goes so far as to serve us. The manner of God's acting—that is, His acting with patience, goodness, compassion, and willingness to make us better people—must also characterize all ministers: Bishops as successors of the Apostles, priests—their co-workers—and deacons who 'serve tables' in practice (Acts 6:2). It is especially deacons who are the face of the Church in the daily life of a community, which lives and journeys in the midst of the people and in which the greatest is not the one who commands, but the one who serves (cf. Lk 22:26)."[178]

Therefore, let's hope that the pope's words can contribute to guiding the processes of self-awareness and evolution of the diaconal ministry.

---

178 Pope Francis, Address to a Delegation of the International Diaconate Center (June 4, 2016).

# The Words of Pope Francis

## Message for the Fifty-Third World Day of Prayer for Vocations

### The Church, Mother of Vocations

*Dear Brothers and Sisters,*

It is my great hope that, during the course of this Extraordinary Jubilee of Mercy, all the baptized may experience the joy of belonging to the Church and rediscover that the Christian vocation, just like every particular vocation, is born from within the People of God, and is a gift of divine mercy. The Church is the house of mercy, and it is the "soil" where vocations take root, mature and bear fruit.

For this reason, on the occasion of the fifty-third World Day of Prayer for Vocations, I invite all of you to reflect upon the apostolic community, and to give thanks for the role of the community in each person's vocational journey. In the Bull of Indiction for the Extraordinary Jubilee of Mercy, I recalled the words of the venerable St. Bede, describing the call of St. Matthew: "*Miserando atque eligendo*" (*Misericordiae Vultus*, no. 8). The Lord's merciful action forgives our sins and opens us to the new life which takes shape in the call to discipleship and mission. Each vocation in the Church has its origin in the compassionate gaze of Jesus. Conversion and vocation are two sides of the same coin, and continually remain interconnected throughout the whole of the missionary disciple's life.

Blessed Paul VI, in his exhortation *Evangelii Nuntiandi*, described various steps in the process of evangelization. One of these steps is belonging to the Christian community (cf. no. 23), that community from which we first received the witness of faith and the clear proclamation of the Lord's mercy. This incorporation into the Christian community brings with it all the richness of ecclesial life, particularly the sacraments. Indeed, the Church is not only a place in which we believe, but it is also an object of our faith; it is for this reason that we profess in the Credo: "I believe in the Church."

The call of God comes to us by means of a *mediation which is communal*. God calls us to become a part of the Church and, after we have reached a certain maturity within it, he bestows on us a specific vocation. The vocational journey is undertaken together with the brothers and sisters whom the Lord has given to us: it is a *con-vocation*. The ecclesial dynamism of the call is an antidote to indifference and to individualism. It establishes the communion in which indifference is vanquished by love, because it demands that we go beyond ourselves and place our lives at the service of God's plan, embracing the historical circumstances of his holy people.

On this day dedicated to prayer for vocations, I urge all the faithful to assume their responsibility for the care and discernment of vocations. When the Apostles sought someone to take the place of Judas Iscariot, St. Peter brought together one hundred and twenty of the brethren (cf. Acts 1:15); and in order to choose seven deacons, a group of disciples was gathered (cf. 6:2). St. Paul gave Titus specific criteria for the selection of presbyters (cf. Ti 1:5-9). Still today, the Christian community is always present in the discernment of vocations, in their formation and in their perseverance (cf. Apost. Ex. *Evangelii Gaudium*, no. 107).

**Vocations are born within the Church**. From the moment a vocation begins to become evident, it is necessary to have an adequate "sense" of the Church. No one is called exclusively for a particular region, or for a group or for an ecclesial movement, but rather for the Church and for the world. "A sure sign of the authenticity of a charism is its ecclesial character, its ability to be integrated harmoniously into the life of God's holy and faithful people for the good of all" (*ibid.*, no. 130).

In responding to God's call, young people see their own ecclesial horizon expand; they are able to consider various charisms and to undertake a more objective discernment. In this way, the community becomes the home and the family where vocations are born. Candidates gratefully contemplate this mediation of the community as an essential element for their future.

They learn to know and to love their brothers and sisters who pursue paths different from their own; and these bonds strengthen in everyone the communion which they share.

**Vocations grow within the Church.** In the course of formation, candidates for various vocations need to grow in their knowledge of the ecclesial community, overcoming the limited perspectives that we all have at the beginning. To that end, it is helpful to undertake *some apostolic experience together with other members of the community*, for example: in the company of a good catechist, to communicate the Christian message; together with a religious community, to experience the evangelization of the peripheries sharing in the life of the cloister, to discover the treasure of contemplation; in contact with missionaries, to know more closely the mission *ad gentes*; and in the company of diocesan priests, to deepen one's experience of pastoral life in the parish and in the diocese. For those who are already in formation, the ecclesial community always remains the fundamental formational environment, toward which one should feel a sense of gratitude.

**Vocations are sustained by the Church.** After definitive commitment, our vocational journey within the Church does not come to an end, but it continues in our willingness to serve, our perseverance and our ongoing formation. The one who has consecrated his life to the Lord is willing to serve the Church wherever it has need.

The mission of Paul and Barnabas is a good example of this readiness to serve the Church. Sent on mission by the Holy Spirit and by the community of Antioch (cf. Acts 13:1-4), they returned to that same community and described what the Lord had worked through them (cf. 14:27). Missionaries are accompanied and sustained by the Christian community, which always remains a vital point of reference, just as a visible homeland offers security to all who are on pilgrimage toward eternal life.

Among those involved in pastoral activity, priests are especially important. In their ministry, they fulfill the words of Jesus, who said: "I am the gate of the sheepfold. . . . I am the good shepherd" (Jn 10:7, 11). The pastoral care of vocations is a fundamental part of their ministry. Priests accompany those who are discerning a vocation, as well as those who have already dedicated their lives to the service of God and of the community.

All the faithful are called to appreciate the ecclesial dynamism of vocations, so that communities of faith can become, after the example of the Blessed Virgin Mary, like a mother's womb which welcomes the gift of the Holy Spirit (cf. Lk 1:35-38). The motherhood of the Church finds expression in constant prayer for vocations and in the work of educating and accompanying all those who perceive God's call. This motherhood is also expressed through a careful selection of candidates for the ordained ministry and for the consecrated life. Finally, the Church is the mother of vocations in her continual support of those who have dedicated their lives to the service of others.

We ask the Lord to grant to all those who are on a vocational journey a deep sense of belonging to the Church; and that the Holy Spirit may strengthen among Pastors, and all of the faithful, a deeper sense of communion, discernment and spiritual fatherhood and motherhood.

Father of mercy, who gave your Son for our salvation and who strengthens us always with the gifts of your Spirit, grant us Christian communities which are alive, fervent and joyous, which are fonts of fraternal life, and which nurture in the young the desire to consecrate themselves to you and to the work of evangelization. Sustain these communities in their commitment to offer appropriate vocational catechesis and ways of proceeding toward each one's particular consecration. Grant the wisdom needed for vocational discernment, so that in all things the greatness of your merciful love may shine forth. May Mary, Mother and guide of Jesus, intercede for each Christian community, so that, made fruitful by the Holy Spirit, it may be a source of true vocations for the service of the holy People of God.

From the Vatican, November 29, 2015

# To a Delegation of the International Diaconate Center

*Dear Brothers and Sisters,*

It's my pleasure to welcome you in occasion of the fiftieth anniversary of the *International Diaconate Center*, which you celebrated at the end of last year. Your visit is taking place during the Holy Year of Mercy, which provides a spiritual context aimed at renewing in us awareness of the importance of mercy in our lives and in our ministry. I thank you all for coming, and I especially thank Msgr. Fürst and Prof. Kiessling for their kind words.

The Lord Jesus entrusted to the Apostles a new Commandment: "love one another, even as I have loved you, that you also love one another" (Jn 13:34). Jesus Himself is this "newness." He gave us an example so that, as He did, we should also do (cf. Jn 13:15). That Commandment of love is the last will of Jesus, given to the disciples in the Upper Room after the washing of their feet. Once again he underlines: "This is my commandment: that you love one another as I have loved you" (Jn 15:12). By loving one another, the disciples continue the mission for which the Son of God came into the world. They understand, with the help of the Holy Spirit, that this Commandment involves service to our brothers and sisters. In order to provide for the concrete care of people and their necessities, the Apostles chose several "deacons," that is, servants. Deacons manifest the Commandment of Jesus in a particular way: imitating God in the service of others; imitating God who is love and even goes so far as to serve us. The manner of God's acting—that is, His acting with patience, goodness, compassion, and willingness to make us better people—must also characterize all ministers: Bishops as successors of the Apostles, priests—their co-workers—and deacons who "serve tables" in practice (Acts 6:2). It is especially deacons who are the face of the Church in the daily life of a community, which lives and journeys in the midst of the people and in which the greatest is not the one who commands, but the one who serves (cf. Lk 22:26).

Dear deacons, I hope your pilgrimage to Rome during this Jubilee Year is an intense experience of the mercy of God and that it helps you to grow in your vocation as ministers of Christ. May the Lord sustain you in your service and help you arrive at an ever deeper faith in His love, so that you may live it in joy and dedication. Know that my prayers and my blessing go with you always and,—please: this is the diaconal service that I ask of you—please do not forget to pray for me.

Saturday, June 4, 2016

# Cathedral of Milan: Encounter with Priests and Consecrated Persons

*Question—Roberto Crespi, Permanent Deacon*

Your Holiness, good morning. I am Roberto, a permanent deacon. The diaconate entered into our clergy 1990, and of whom there are now 143 of us; it is not a large number but it is a significant number. We are men who live their vocation fully; either in marriage or celibacy, but we also live fully in the world of work and of the professions, and therefore bring the clergy into the world of families and the world of work, we bring all those dimensions of beauty and experience but also hardship and at times suffering. So, we ask you: as permanent deacons, what is our role in giving form to the face [of the] Church that is humble, that is selfless, that is blessed, that we feel she is in her heart, and of which often you speak to us? Thank you for your attention, and I assure you of our prayer, and that of our wives and families.

*Pope Francis*

Thank you. You deacons have much to give, much to give. I think of the value of discernment. Within the presbytery, you can be an authoritative voice to show the tension there is between duty and will, the tensions that one lives in family life—you have a mother-in-law, for example! And also the blessings one lives within family life.

But we must be careful not to see deacons as half priests, half laypeople. This is a danger. At the end they will end up neither one nor the other. No, we must not do this, it is a danger. Looking at them in this way harms us and harms them. This way of considering them takes strength from the charism proper to the diaconate. I want to return to this: the charism proper to the diaconate. And this charism is in the life of the Church. Likewise the image of the deacon as a sort of intermediary between the faithful and pastors is inappropriate. Neither halfway between priests and laypeople, nor halfway between pastors and faithful. There is the danger of clericalism: the deacon who is too clerical. No, no, this is not good. At times I see someone who assists at the liturgy: it almost seems as if he wants to take the place of the priest. Clericalism, beware of clericalism. And another temptation is functionalism: it is a help that the priest has for this or that; a boy to carry out certain tasks and not for other things. No. You have a clear charism in the Church and you must build it.

The diaconate is a specific vocation, a family vocation that requires service. I like it very much when [in the Acts of the Apostles] the first Hellenistic Christians went to the apostles to complain because their widows and orphans were not well cared for, and they had a meeting, that "synod" between apostles and disciples, and they "invented" the deacons to serve. And this is very interesting for us bishops too, because they were all bishops, those who "made" the deacons. And what does this tell us? That deacons were servants. Then they understood that, in that case, it was to assist widows and orphans: but to serve. And to us as bishops: prayer and the proclamation of the Word; and this shows us what the most important charism of a bishop is: to pray. What is the task of a bishop, the first task? Prayer. Second task: proclaiming the Word. But you can see the difference clearly. And for you [deacons]: service. This word is the key to understanding your charism. Service as one of the characteristic gifts of the people of God. The deacon is, so to say, the custodian of service in the Church. Every word must be carefully measured. You are the guardians of service in the Church: service to the Word, service to the Altar, service to the poor. And your mission, the mission of the deacon, and your contribution consist in this: in reminding us all that faith, in its various expressions—community liturgy, personal prayer, the various forms of charity—and in its various states of life—lay, clerical, family—possesses an essential dimension of service. Service to God and to brothers. And how far we have to go in this sense! You are the guardians of service in the Church.

Therein lies the value of the charisms in the Church, which are a memory and a gift for helping all the people of God not to lose the perspective and wealth of God's action. You are not half priests, half laypeople—this would be to "functionalize" the diaconate—you are the sacrament of service to God and to others. And from this word "service" there derives all the development of your work, of your vocation, of your being within the Church. A vocation that, like all vocations, is not only individual but lived within the family and with the family; within the People of God and with the People of God.

In summary:

- there is no altar service, there is no liturgy that is not open to the poor, and there is no service to the poor that does not lead to the liturgy;
- there is no ecclesial vocation that is not of the family.

This helps us to reevaluate the diaconate as an ecclesial vocation.

Finally, today it seems that everything must be useful to us, as if everything were targeted at the individual: prayer is useful to me, the community is useful to me, charity is useful to me. This is a feature of our culture. You are the gift that the Spirit gives us to show that the right path goes in the opposite direction: in prayer I serve, in the community I serve, with solidarity I serve God and my neighbor. And may God give you the grace to grow in this charism of safeguarding service in the Church. Thank you for what you do.

Saturday, March 25, 2017

# PART XI
# The Diaconia of Preaching

Another feature that has distinguished the Church's reflection on the diaconate is the service of the Word and of preaching.

In the *Instrumentum Laboris* from the Synod on the New Evangelization, the following question is formulated: *In what way has the ministry of the diaconate found an element of its identity in the evangelizing mandate?*

If the Church is generated by the Paschal Mystery of the Eucharist, then we can see how the deacon, through his service at the altar and to the poor, becomes the concrete and undeniable meeting point between liturgical-Eucharistic service, which is the source of every diaconia, and the concrete life of each New Testament community. However, the Eucharist is composed of two inseparable "tables" that the actions of the deacon have the task of realizing in liturgy, as in life. The only way that the People of God and the world will understand that ministerial diaconia is different from philanthropy, or from any other form of generic solidarity, will be through the unselfish authenticity of the service of deacons and the wisdom of their word of consolation. As the liturgical signs performed by the deacon during the

Eucharistic celebration indicate, Gospel proclamation and dispensing the chalice are not only the source and point of arrival of his diaconia but also the normative exemplification that should inspire his conduct.

If service at the table, which is rendered first to brothers then to all the poor, is derived by natural sacramental expansion from the diaconia of the Eucharist, then from *diaconia verbi* comes a true ministry of the Word that finds its biblical source and precise ecclesial identity in the evangelization of the least and the marginalized. Indeed, the deacon is a "teacher insofar as he preaches and bears witness the Word of God; he sanctifies when he administers the Sacrament of Baptism, the Holy Eucharist and the Sacramentals; . . . he is a guide inasmuch as he animates the community or a section of ecclesial life."[179] Like the priestly order, diaconal service is made up of teaching, sanctifying, and guiding. This is why our bishops have always considered it fundamental to the ordained diaconia to recognize the deacon's concrete ability to be the animator of the service of the Word, not only of the Liturgy and charity, in the community to which he belongs.

The concrete ways in which the ministry of the Word is exercised have required more intense biblical and theological preparation and the adequate spiritual formation of candidates. In recent years, this has meant putting

---

179 *Directory*, no. 22.

progressively more emphasis on the formative period of the diaconal process. This theological and spiritual formation should be aimed at leading to a more personal knowledge of the figure of Christ the servant, as opposed to approving courses of study with other objectives, such as the teaching of religion in schools. We must seek with love and discipline to know the exemplarity of Christ by practicing the *lectio divina*—which is strongly recommended by the Church and John Paul II—to reiterate the primacy of the Word that is presented as an ordinary place and a real occasion for diaconal ministeriality. It is significant that it is emphasized more than once and in many different documents that Gospel proclamation requires deacons to have a sincere and faithful love of the Word, but also to engage in effective evangelizing work. This work can be realized in the different forms of catechesis (from the preparation of the sacraments to the so-called catechesis of adults, meetings with struggling couples, and conversations with nonbelievers and non-Christians), but it cannot be reduced to the liturgical proclamation of the Gospel alone.

Many documents from local churches reiterate that when the primacy of Scripture is real, it tends to leaven from docile and assiduous listening to personal participation in the liturgical season of prayer, to then find its final landing place in the diaconia of the Word. Many documents assign a special place in this pedagogy of listening to and proclaiming the Word to the community preparation of the Sunday liturgy and to the studying/ praying of the Sunday readings. This highlights the fact that, apart from being a natural place for *diaconia verbi*, this ancient form of sanctification of the Day of the Lord can also be an occasion to discern the candidate's aptitude to carry out an effective ministry of the Word. This form of diaconia of the Word can assume the appearance of a true vigil Liturgy: it can be organized in the Church on Saturday evening and involve the entire community, or it can simply be carried out in homes, especially as a way to facilitate the participation of individuals, especially those who are far away and marginalized, and their families and friends.

# The Words of Pope Francis

## Apostolic Exhortation *Evangelii Gaudium*, on the Proclamation of the Gospel in Today's World

### Chapter Three

### The Proclamation of the Gospel

### III. *Preparing to Preach*

159. Another feature of a good homily is that it is positive. It is not so much concerned with pointing out what shouldn't be done, but with suggesting what we can do better. In any case, if it does draw attention to something negative, it will also attempt to point to a positive and attractive value, lest it remain mired in complaints, laments, criticisms and reproaches. Positive preaching always offers hope, points to the future, does not leave us trapped in negativity. How good it is when priests, deacons and the laity gather periodically to discover resources which can make preaching more attractive!

Given in Rome, at St. Peter's, on November 24, the Solemnity of Our Lord Jesus Christ, King of the Universe, and the conclusion of the Year of Faith, in the year 2013, the first of my Pontificate

# PART XII
# The Diaconia of Women

"A Church without women"—Pope Francis said on his way back from Rio—"is like the college of the Apostles without Mary. The role of women in the Church is not simply that of maternity, being mothers, but much greater: it is precisely to be the icon of the Virgin, of Our Lady; what helps make the Church grow! But think about it, Our Lady is more important than the Apostles! She is more important! The Church is feminine. She is Church, she is bride, she is mother . . . the role of women in the Church must not be limited to being mothers, workers, a limited role . . . No! It is something else! . . . Paul VI wrote beautifully of women, but I believe that we have much more to do in making explicit this role and charism of women. We can't imagine a Church without women, but women active in the Church, with the distinctive role that they play. . . . In the Church, this is how we should think of women: taking risky decisions, yet as women. This needs to be better explained. I believe that we have not yet come up with a profound theology of womanhood, in the Church. All we say is: they can do this, they can do that, now they are altar servers, now they do the readings, they are in charge of Caritas (Catholic charities)."[180]

Since the beginning of his papacy, Jorge Mario Bergoglio has declared his intention to promote the role of women. In the famous interview six months after the Conclave, he told the director of *La Civiltà Cattolica*, Fr. Antonio Spadaro, that "the feminine genius is needed wherever we make important decisions. The challenge today is this: to think about the specific place of women also in those places where the authority of the church is exercised for various areas of the church."[181]

The pope presented the idea of a commission to study the possibility of a female diaconate in his meeting with the International Union of Superiors General on May 12, 2016, in the Vatican. The following question was asked by a woman religious in the closed-door interview, which was first reported by the Catholic press from the United States and then published in *L'Osservatore Romano*: "In the Church there is the office of the permanent diaconate, but it is open only to men, married or not. What prevents the Church from including women among permanent deacons, as was the case in

---

180  Pope Francis, In-Flight Press Conference (July 28, 2013).

181  Antonio Spadaro, SJ, "A Big Heart Open to God: An Interview with Pope Francis," *America Magazine* (September 30, 2013).

the primitive Church? Why not constitute an official commission to study the matter?"[182]

Francis's answer was clear: "I remember that it was a theme which interested me considerably when I came to Rome for meetings, and I stayed at the *Domus Paolo VI*; there was a good Syrian theologian there, who had produced a critical edition and translation of the Hymns of Ephrem the Syrian. One day I asked him about this, and he explained to me that in the early times of the Church there were some deaconesses. But what were these deaconesses? Were they ordained or not? The Council of Chalcedon (in 451) speaks about this, but it is somewhat unclear. What was the role of deaconesses in those times? It seems—I was told by this man, who is now dead but who was a good professor, wise and erudite—it seems that the role of the deaconesses was to help in the baptism of women, with their immersion; for the sake of decorum they baptized them; and also anointed the body of women, in baptism. And another curious fact: when there was a judgment on a marriage because a husband beat his wife and she went to the bishop to lay a complaint, deaconesses were responsible for inspecting the bruises left on the woman's body from her husband's blows, and for informing the bishop. This I remember. There are various publications on the diaconate in the Church, but it is not clear how it was in the past. I think

---

182 Pope Francis, Address to the International Union of Superiors General (May 12, 2016).

I will ask the Congregation for the Doctrine of the Faith to refer me to some studies on this theme, because I have answered you only on the basis of what I heard from this priest, who was a learned and good researcher, on the permanent diaconate. In addition, I would like to constitute an official commission to study the question: I think it will be good for the Church to clarify this point; I agree, and I will speak [to the Congregation] in order to do something of this nature."

The pope returned to this topic on June 26 of that same year in response to a question from journalists who were accompanying him on his flight back from his recent trip to Armenia. He lamented how the matter had been reported in newspapers ("The next day: . . . 'Church opens the door to women deacons!' To tell the truth, I was a little annoyed with the media because this is not telling people the whole truth") and explained: "I spoke with the Prefect of the Congregation for the Doctrine of the Faith, who told me: 'But there was a study done by the International Theological Commission in the 1980s.' I spoke with the president of the Superiors General and told her: 'Please give me a list of persons you think could be on this commission.' And she sent me the list. The Prefect also sent a list, and they are on my desk, with a view to establishing this commission. I believe that much attention was given to the issue back in the 80s and it will not be difficult to shed light on the matter."[183]

So, are women deacons a possibility? It is certainly a good opportunity for us to take another look at the value of the ministeriality of the entire Church of Christian men and women as well as the value of the rethinking of the ordained ministry. While "the feminine genius" has been mentioned frequently in recent decades in sermons, the catechesis, and magisterial documents, today it seems urgent that we rethink the forms and structures of ecclesial life so that spaces for participation and places of decision-making can finally be occupied by women and so the elaboration of theological thought and pastoral choices at all levels can be marked by the influential, public, and competent word of women. Thus, reflection is focused on current matter within the broader horizon of Tradition, but it also urges us to seriously rethink a chapter of history that is little known, one that is filled with female ministerial figures who enriched the life of the early Christian Church in many ways. We are also urged to reflect on the future of a Church that is truly a community of men and women. The discussion on the diaconate has been documented in the *Traditio Ecclesiae* and referenced in many ecumenical dialogues. It was reconsidered in light of the theology of the ministry of the Council and today, it is actively sought and also

---

183 Pope Francis, In-Flight Press Conference (June 26, 2016).

becomes a possible path, not in the form of an unoriginal re-proposing of the past (which would be anachronistic), but as a ministry of women and by women for today's Church. So, the time has come for the Church to listen to the word and to see the work of women who, as the funeral inscription of Aeria, deacon of Amisos (†562), says are "faithful servant[s] of Christ, deacon[s] of saints, friend[s] to all."

# The Words of Pope Francis

## Audience with the International Union of Superiors General

## Interview with the Holy Father

*First Question*

*For a Better Integration of Women in the Life of the Church*

Pope Francis, you said that "the feminine genius is needed in all expressions in the life of society . . . and in the Church," and yet women are excluded from decision-making processes in the Church, especially at the highest levels, and from preaching at the Eucharist. An important obstacle to the Church's full embrace of "feminine genius" is the bond that decision-making processes and preaching both have with priestly ordination. Do you see a way of separating leadership roles and preaching at the Eucharist from ordination, so that our Church can be more open to receiving the genius of women in the very near future?

We must distinguish between various things here. The question is linked to functionality, it is closely linked to functionality, while the role of women goes beyond this. But I will answer the question now, then let us speak . . . I have seen that there are other questions that go beyond this.

It is true that women are excluded from decision-making processes in the Church: not excluded, but the presence of women is very weak there, in decision-making processes. We must move forward. For example—truly I see no difficulty—I believe that in the Pontifical Council for Justice and Peace the secretariat is managed by a woman religious. Another was proposed and I appointed her but she preferred not to accept as she had to go elsewhere to do other work in her congregation. We must move forward, because for many aspects of decision-making processes ordination is not necessary. It is not necessary. In the reform of the Apostolic Constitution *Pastor Bonus*, speaking of Dicasteries, when there is no jurisdiction deriving from ordination—that is, pastoral jurisdiction—it is not written that it can be a woman, I don't know about a head of a Dicastery, but . . . For example, for migrants: a woman could go to the Dicastery for Migrants. And when it is necessary—now that migrants fall under the jurisdiction of a Dicastery, it will be for the Prefect to give this permission. But ordinarily, in the execution of a decision-making process, this can be done. For me the process leading to decisions is very important: not only the execution, but also the development, and therefore that women, whether consecrated or lay, become part of the reflection process and part of the discussion. Because women look at life through their own eyes and we men are not able to look at life in this way. The way of viewing a problem, of seeing anything, is different for a woman compared to a man. They must be complementary, and in consultations it is important that there are women.

I experienced a problem in Buenos Aires: looking at it with the priests' council—therefore all men—it was well handled, but then looking at the matter with a group of religious and lay women brought great benefit, and this helped the decision by offering a complementary view. This is really necessary! And I think we must move forward on this; then the decision-making process can be examined.

There is also the problem of preaching at the Eucharistic Celebration. There is no problem for a woman—religious or lay—to preach in the Liturgy of the Word. There is no problem. But at the Eucharistic Celebration there is a liturgical-dogmatic problem, because it is one celebration—the Liturgy of the Word and the Eucharistic Liturgy, there is unity between them—and the one who presides over it is Jesus Christ. The priest or bishop who presides does so in the person of Jesus Christ. It is a theological-liturgical reality. In that situation, there being no women's ordination, they cannot preside. But it is possible to study and explain further what I have just said very quickly and rather simply.

With *leadership*, on the other hand, there is no problem: we must go forward in that area, prudently, but seeking solutions . . .

Now there are two temptations here, against which we must guard.

The first is feminism: the woman's role in the Church is not one of feminism; it is a right! It is a right as a baptized person, with the charisms and the gifts that the Spirit has given. We must not fall into feminism, because this would reduce a woman's importance. I do not see, at this moment, a great danger of this among women religious. I do not see that. Perhaps in the past, but in general it is not present.

The other danger, a very strong temptation I have spoken of several times, is clericalism. And this is very strong. Let us consider that today more than 60 percent of parishes—of dioceses I don't know, but only a little fewer—do not have a finance or a pastoral council. What does this mean? It means that the parish or diocese is led with a clerical spirit, by the priest alone, and that it does not implement synodality in the parish, in the diocese, which is not a novelty under this Pope. No! It is a matter of Canon Law: the parish priest is obliged to have a council of laypeople, for and with lay men, women and women religious for pastoral ministry and financial affairs. And they do not do this. This is the danger of clericalism in the Church today. We must go ahead and remove this danger, because the priest is a servant of the community, the bishop is a servant of the community, but he is not the head of a firm. No! This is important. In Latin America, for example, clericalism is very strong and pronounced. Laypeople do not know what to do, if they do not ask the priest. It is very strong. And for this reason, awareness of the laity's role has been very delayed. This is saved just a little through popular piety, since the protagonist here is the people, and the people have done things as they thought best. Priests have not taken much interest in this regard; some have not viewed this phenomenon of popular piety favorably. But clericalism is a negative attitude. And it requires complicity: it is something done by two parties, just as it takes two to dance the tango . . . That is: the priest wants to clericalize the layman, the laywoman, the man or woman religious, and the layperson asks to be clericalized, because it is easier that way. And this is odd. In Buenos Aires I experienced this on three or four occasions: a good priest came to me and said, "I have an excellent layman in my parish: he does this and that, he knows how to organize things, he gets things done; he is a man of real integrity . . . Shall we make him a deacon?" Or rather, shall we "clericalize" him? "No! Let him remain a layman. Don't make him a deacon." This is important. You have this experience that clericalism often hampers things from developing correctly.

I will ask—and perhaps I will get this to the President—the Congregation for Divine Worship to explain properly and in depth what I said rather briefly on preaching in the Eucharistic Celebration, as I do not have sufficient theology or clarity to explain it now. But we must distinguish clearly: preaching at a Liturgy of the Word is one thing, and this can be done; but the Eucharistic Celebration is something else: here there is a different mystery. It is the mystery of Christ's presence, and the priest or the bishop celebrates *in persona Christi*. For *leadership* it is clear . . . Yes, I think this could be my general answer to the first question.

## Second Question

### The Role of Consecrated Women in the Church

Consecrated women already do much work with the poor and the marginalized, they teach catechism, they accompany the sick and the dying, they distribute Communion; in many countries they lead the communal prayers in the absence of a priest and in those circumstances they give a homily. In the Church there is the office of the permanent diaconate, but it is open only to men, married or not. What prevents the Church from including women among permanent deacons, as was the case in the primitive Church? Why not constitute an official commission to study the matter? Can you give us an example of where you see the possibility of better integration of women and consecrated women in the life of the Church?

## Pope Francis

This question goes in the direction of "doing": consecrated women already do much work with the poor, they do many things . . . "doing." And it touches on the problem of the permanent diaconate. Some might say that the "permanent deaconesses" in the life of the Church are mothers-in-law [laughter]. Indeed this existed in early times: there was a beginning . . . I remember that it was a theme which interested me considerably when I came to Rome for meetings, and I stayed at the *Domus Paolo VI*; there was a good Syrian theologian there, who had produced a critical edition and translation of the Hymns of Ephrem the Syrian. One day I asked him about this, and he explained to me that in the early times of the Church there were some deaconesses. But what were these deaconesses? Were they ordained or not? The Council of Chalcedon (in 451) speaks about this, but it is somewhat unclear. What was the role of deaconesses in those times? It seems—I was told by this man, who is now dead but who was a good professor, wise and erudite—it seems that the role of the deaconesses was to help in the baptism of women, with their immersion; for the sake of decorum they baptized them; and also anointed the body of women, in baptism. And another curious fact: when there was a judgment on a marriage because a husband beat his wife and she went to the bishop to lay a complaint, deaconesses were responsible for inspecting the bruises left on the woman's body from her husband's blows, and for informing the bishop. This I remember. There are various publications on the diaconate in the Church, but it is not clear how it was in the past. I think I will ask the Congregation for the Doctrine of the Faith to refer me to some studies on this theme, because I have answered you only on the basis of what I heard from this priest, who was a learned and good researcher, on the permanent diaconate. In addition, I would like to constitute an official commission to study the question: I think it will be good for the Church to clarify this point; I agree, and I will speak [to the Congregation] in order to do something of this nature.

Then you say: "We agree with you, Holy Father, that you have on several occasions raised the issue of the need for a more incisive role for women in decision-making roles in the Church." This is clear. "Can you give me an example of where you see the possibility of better integration of women and of consecrated women in the life of the Church?" I will say something afterward, because I have seen that there is a general question. In the consultations of the Congregation for Religious, in the assemblies, women religious must be present: this is true. In consultations on so many problems which get presented, consecrated women must be present. Another thing: improved integration. At the moment specific examples do not come to mind, but there is still what I said earlier: seeking out the judgment of consecrated women, because women see things with an originality different to that of men; and this is enriching, in consultation, and decision-making, and in practice.

This work that you carry out with the poor, the marginalized, teaching catechism, accompanying the sick and the dying, this is very "maternal" work, where the maternity of the Church is expressed the most. But there are men who do the same, and that's fine: consecrated men, hospitaller orders . . . and that is important.

So then, with regard to the diaconate, yes, I think that it is useful to have a commission that clarifies this area properly, especially with regard to the early times of the Church.

With regard to improved integration, I repeat what I said earlier.

If there is something [that] needs to be explained in more detail, please ask me now: are there any further questions on what I have said, that may help me to think? Let's go on.

Vatican City, Thursday, May 12, 2016

# PART XIII
# A Diaconal Church
## *The Preferential Option for the Poor*

In his message for the First World Day of the Poor,—which he instituted at the end of the Jubilee of Mercy and which was celebrated on November 19, 2017—Pope Francis proposed the theme "Let us love, not with words but with deeds," which summarizes his entire apostolate. The opening sentence, with its call for concreteness: "Little children, let us not love in word or speech, but in deed and in truth (1 Jn 3:18),"[184] echoes what he said in Florence to bishops and the Italian Church: "Not putting into practice, not leading the Word into reality, means building on sand, staying within pure idea and decaying into intimisms that bear no fruit, that render its dynamism barren."[185] The pope touches on all of the sensitive topics that have already been addressed in the documents of his Magisterium. The poor are people to meet, embrace, and love. Pope Francis reminds us that poverty is not an abstract entity, but "has the face of

---

184 Pope Francis, Message for the First World Day of the Poor (June 13, 2017).

185 Pope Francis, Address (November 10, 2015).

women, men and children exploited by base interests, crushed by the machinations of power and money. What a bitter and endless list we would have to compile were we to add the poverty born of social injustice, moral degeneration, the greed of a chosen few, and generalized indifference!"[186] It is a poverty that "stifles the spirit of initiative of so many young people by keeping them from finding work." In the face of these situations, the pope asks us not to be inactive and resigned, but to "respond with a new vision of life and society."

# [Transcript][187]

More than fifty years have passed since the signing of the historic Pact of the Catacombs (November 16, 1965) in the Catacombs of St. Domitilla in Rome. The Pact was simply a pledge that was signed by forty bishops participating in Vatican II to live the simple life of the people, renouncing every form of power, richness, and privilege: "We will seek to live according to the ordinary manner of our people, regarding habitation, food, means of transport and

---

186 Pope Francis, Message for the First World Day of the Poor.

187 Fr. Mariano Tibaldo, "The Preferential Choice of the Poor and Social Commitment in the Institute of the Comboni Missionaries," January 18, 2016. Originally published in Italian as *"La scelta preferenziale dei poveri e l'impegno sociale nell'Istituto dei Missionari Comboniani,"* Missionari Comboniani, *http://www.comboni.org/contenuti/107922* (assessed May 3, 2018).

all which springs from this. We definitively renounce the appearance and reality of riches, especially regarding to our manner of dress (rich material, loud colors). . . . We will not possess real estate, goods, bank accounts etc. in our own names." Furthermore, the bishops committed to taking political action within governments to create structures of justice, equality, and development, to freeing themselves of the financial administration of the diocese, which they would entrust to the laity in order to have more time for pastoral work and serving the poor, and to sharing their lives with priests, religious, and laity. In short, it was a historic and, at the time, greatly prophetic commitment of a few bishops that made poverty and sobriety a dimension of their lives and that made the poor the priority of their apostolic and pastoral service.

The bishops who signed the Pact—which included the likes of Hélder Câmara, Leonidas Proaño, Antonio Fragoso, José Maria Pires, Luigi Bettazzi, and the Argentinian bishop Enrique Angelelli (assassinated in 1976)—were part of an informal group that gathered in the Belgian College beginning in 1962 on the topic of the "Church of the Poor." This group, which was led by Charles M. Himmer, bishop of Tournai, was inspired by the theology of Paul Gauthier and the Carmelite woman religious Marie-Thérèse Lescase. The group took its name from the words of Pope John XXIII, who declared in a radio message on September 11, 1962, one month after the beginning of the Council: "With respect to the underdeveloped countries, the Church appears as it is and wants to be: the Church of all people and, in particular, the Church of the poor."

However, the Second Vatican Council did not give particular attention to the topic of the poverty of the Church, despite the insistence of Cardinal Giacomo Lercaro, who would have liked for the poor and the poverty of the Church to be the Council's main focus. Lercaro's appeal did, however, appear in *Lumen Gentium*, number 8.3, which says that the Church "in the poor and afflicted sees the image of its poor and suffering Founder. It does all it can to relieve their need and in them it strives to serve Christ"—but the revolutionary significance of that sentence did not have a great effect on pastoral working, nor was it truly assimilated. Moreover, Paul VI feared that the issue of poverty might have political repercussions (those were the days of the Cold War and the fear of communism); the pope, however, did commit to taking Msgr. Lercaro's suggestions at a later time, after the conciliar event. This commitment took the form of an encyclical, *Populorum Progressio*.

However, in the Second General Conference of the Latin American Episcopate in Medellín

(Colombia) in 1968, the poverty of the Church was addressed in detail, and the Church's work was devised to start with the poor, who were to be considered in their existential poverty. The final document reads: "The poverty of the church and of its members in Latin America ought to be a sign and a commitment—a sign of the inestimable value of the poor in the eyes of God, an obligation of solidarity with those who suffer" (XIV, 7). "Evangelization needs the support of a Church that is a sign" (VII, 13). In the Third General Conference in Puebla, Mexico, in 1979, one of the criteria and signs of evangelization will be "preferential love and concern for the poor and needy" (no. 381).

The Pact of the Catacombs is of epochal significance because it breaks away from the Constantinian alliance of throne and altar and becomes the hermeneutical key of a Church that wants to free itself from getting mixed up with power and prestige. The commitment that, in the pact's original intentions, was limited to the personal choice of a few bishops, would, in the years to come, become a challenge for the entire Church: poverty as a dimension proper to her life and the poor as the preferential option, an option that is theological and, at the same time, Christological because, as Pope Benedict XVI said, "the option for the poor is rooted in faith in the God who became poor in

Christ." This challenge still struggles to become a reality, but nevertheless, it has become an integral part of the Church's self-awareness. This is the challenge of Pope Francis: "I want a Church which is poor and for the poor."[188]

# [Transcript][189]

The Apostolic Exhortation *Evangelii Gaudium* contains many aspects having to do with the social doctrine of the Church both directly and indirectly. It is a text marked by the centrality of the encounter with Jesus Christ, the Savior and the Merciful One, in the life of each Christian. The "joy" of which Pope Francis speaks is not a generic psychological sentiment; it is the joy of the person saved, salvation encountered and experienced in the life of grace, the mercy that forgives us our sins if we also so wish, and the light that faith in Jesus Christ shines on our life as a whole, our personal, family, community and social life. It is a "Christocentric" apostolic exhortation

---

188 EG, no. 198.

189 Archbishop-Bishop of Trieste Giampaolo Crepaldi, "*Evangelii Gaudium* and the Social Doctrine of the Church," February 12, 2013. Originally published in Italian as "*Evangelii gaudium e la dottrina sociale della chiesa,*" *La Stampa, http://www.lastampa.it/2013/12/02/vaticaninsider/evangelii-gaudium-e-la-dottrina-sociale-della-chiesa-dnEd98oQK-Wis7cZEOjmWwO/pagina.html* (accessed May 3, 2018).

because the light of Jesus Christ is the source of light for creation, the Church, humanity, and history.

This Christocentric approach is very important also for the social doctrine of the Church, which, as repeatedly taught by John Paul II, is "the announcement of Christ in temporal realities," and only in this light does it deal with everything else. It is likewise important because it entails, among other things, the priority of announcement over denouncement. This too is an underlying approach already present in the social teaching of the Church, which Pope Francis now takes up anew and further develops.

The announcement must be made with joy because at its origin is a "yes" that comes well before any critical observation about social conditions today. In the beginning there is the announcement of salvation, mercy, and justice. . . .

The themes and the global perspective of the social doctrine of the Church are present throughout the exhortation, but are concentrated especially in Chapters II and IV. In the latter chapter entitled "The Social Dimension of Evangelization" the Holy Father uses fresh language in highlighting the major themes of the relationship between the announcement of Christ and its community repercussions, between the confession of faith and social commitment, but also announces new perspectives that enrich the previous Magisterium: "time is greater than space," "unity prevails over conflict," "realities are greater than ideas," "the whole is greater than the part." These constitute four new perspectives to be used as a basis for rethinking social relations as a whole.

Once again regarding the social doctrine of the Church, an additional new development to be found in *Evangelii Gaudium* is the in-depth treatment of the "preferential choice for the poor" to be found in Chapter IV. The Holy Father speaks about it from the viewpoint of the evangelical love of Jesus for the little ones and the last of the last, and what he has to say abounds with food for thought and reflection regarding the attitude of both believers and the Church toward the poor, as well as just how much can be learned from them. Presented in these terms, the social inclusion of the poor becomes something more than a mere social policy. It becomes the selfsame perspective of our living in society, the aspect or feature that never ceases to remind us about the ultimate motive for there being a political community. In an explicit or implicit fashion, present in one form or another is all the thinking of the social doctrine of the Church on solidarity and the common good, but this time around from the viewpoint of the poor. In this regard we are now living a particular moment in time. The economic crisis is causing an increase in the forms and magnitude of inequalities, and therefore in the numbers of poor persons and the extent of poverty as such. A new gaze brought to bear on the poor from the viewpoint of the poor understood in an evangelical sense will be certainly be a great help for one and all.

Among the many ideas and entreaties in *Evangelii Gaudium* emerges the important concept of "peace in society," which the Holy Father explains further in Chapter IV. There is diplomatic peace among nations, political peace among political parties, but there is also social peace among social classes and among citizens. Very little thought is given to this, even though today it is the most disruptive element of all, as inequalities and job insecurity end up pitting citizens and entire social groups against one another. In this regard, the exhortation contains some healthy provocations directed toward the economy and politics, urging them to place the human person and authentic common good once again at the heart of their affairs. *Evangelii Gaudium* has a strongly missionary aspect due to the Christocentric approach mentioned earlier. Pope Francis calls on the Church at large to have the courage of the mission and to overcome paralyzing factors such as inertia and excessive scruples.

This is also true for the social doctrine of the Church. In *Centesimus Annus*, John Paul II wrote that this social doctrine has a "concrete" and "experiential" aspect, and he called on all believers to become courageously proactive in their own right, becoming part of the stream of people who, from the very beginning of the Church, have labored intensely for the common good of their brothers and sisters. The fact that the Church should go out of herself for the mission does not mean we have to leave churches empty or abandon doctrine and the sacramental life. According to Pope Francis, it means we must always let ourselves be guided by what is essential, and in the life of the Christian, that which is essential must be given to all.

In order to integrate the commentary on the apostolic exhortation given above, let's indicate some of the most important points from the chapter on the inclusion of the poor in society. The immediacy of the text and the simplicity with which these points are expressed require no further analysis or explanation.

# The Eye of the Church on the Poor

If this way of being a Church, of being a ministry at the service of the world and above all, of the poor and the oppressed, is truly the work of the Spirit, then it requires sacrifice and suffering from us. Far from being discouraged by the opposition from without and within, we should rejoice with the Apostles for being able to suffer for the coming of the Kingdom.

Let us take inspiration from Paul's example: How much was he made to suffer by his Jewish brothers, and even Christians, in order to free the young Church from the yoke of Jewish law?

We too must free our communities from everything that keeps them from putting themselves totally at the service of Christ in the world, at the service of the poor.

As deacons, we will be the first to suffer because we must be the sign and the instrument of this renewal. But we must not be afraid, because the Lord is with us and his victory passes through the Cross!

But the restoration of the permanent diaconate is even a sign that the Church herself gives to illustrate her mission in a concrete way. This brings us to the central purpose of diaconal service. In this way, we can see even more clearly what the specific nature of the diaconal office is made of. The Christological roots of the diaconal office are very deep. This is exemplified in the activity and death of St. Stephen, who, by no accident, is the protomartyr and protodeacon. Herein lies the permanent heart of the "office" that is always present, even in the other ministries.

It seems to have been mainly the tradition of an ancient Syriac ecclesial arrangement that preserved this spiritual aspect of the deacon.

First, let him do only those things which are commanded by the bishop as for proclamation; and let him be the counsellor of the whole clergy, and the mystery of the Church; who ministereth to the sick, who ministereth to the strangers, who helpeth the widows, who is the father of the orphans, who goeth about all the houses of those that are in need, lest any be in affliction or sickness or misery. Let him go about in the houses of the catechumens, so that he may confirm those who are doubting and teach those who are unlearned. Let him clothe those men who have departed, adorning [them]; burying the strangers; guiding those who pass from their dwelling, or go into captivity. For the help of those who are in need let him notify the Church; let him not trouble the bishop; but only on the first day of the week let him make mention about everything, so that he may know[190]

This text puts before our eyes the entire range of the deacon's service, which is without limits. In this ancient ecclesial arrangement, the deacon's tasks range from finding and burying bodies after shipwrecks to testifying to the loyalty and honesty of a raped woman. There is

190 James Cooper and Arthur John Maclean, translators, *The Testament of Our Lord*, translated into English from the Syriac with Introduction and Notes, chapter 34, "Deacons" (Eugene, Oregon: WIPF and Stock, 2008—previously published by T & T Clark, 1902) 97-98.

also the beautiful expression that says the deacon must *be in everything as the eye of the Church.*

This expression is not talking about an eye like that of a guardian, but rather the sensitive perception of suffering and need that comes from authentic closeness and fraternal solidarity. And so, the eye of the deacon continually expands the horizons of the Church and senses suffering and needs in the most hidden corners of the community and at its borders. Throughout the reality of our communities, there are dark areas and there are luminous areas. The edifying role of the deacon in his community requires him to perceive the suffering and needs that are present in the community and, as much as possible, to spread the mercy of Jesus Christ in a concrete way, making it visible to man. His specific responsibility for wayfarers, strangers, and those without a homeland makes needs present to the community, needs that absolutely exist today.

Perhaps it is here that we can best understand the reason why diaconia expresses the essence of ministry and the essence of the Church in such an original way. When he fulfills his most profound task, the deacon is a figure of pure service. He represents the love of Jesus Christ toward all men in a way that is full, so to speak, and not watered down with other tasks, and therefore, in a way that is particularly credible. Before the Church takes any direct action, she must represent the love of the One who came not to be served, but to serve (cf.

Mk 10:45). In this respect, the deacon represents something crucial and unique for the Christian message. This is also why it makes sense to have the three parts of ecclesial ministry. *Whoever holds a superior office in the Church must have lived the fundamental attitude of pure service for a period of time in the diaconal service in a way that is still "pure" (without the "temptation of power") so that he remains marked for life when he moves on to higher levels of service in the Church.*

Naturally, traditional language lends itself to misunderstandings, even if it is used to express something correct. This happens, for example, in speaking about a lower degree of the hierarchy or about steps in general. Jesus is extremely critical when his Apostles argue over precedence. His response is particularly drastic: "You know that those who are recognized as rulers over the Gentiles lord it over them, and their great ones make their authority over them felt. But it shall not be so among you. Rather, whoever wishes to be great among you will be your servant [*diákonos*]; whoever wishes to be first among you will be the slave [*doulos*] of all" (Mk 10:42-44 ff.). Jesus tells his Apostles to serve, not to command, and bears witness to his law with his own behavior. Indeed, the "lowest place" is the most prestigious. Here we are talking about a "career 'toward the bottom.'"

At this point, we must also respond to the many questions that come to mind regarding the restoration of the permanent diaconate. Are permanent deacons really instituted in relation to their original task? Or are they essentially being used, within the framework of the needs that do, in fact, exist in our communities, to make up for the reduction in priestly vocations? But we are also being asked whether or not we are setting, and have set, the right priorities in our communities. What value does diaconia have for us that cannot simply be covered by the highly meritorious work of Caritas [Catholic Charities]? Today there are duties and functions of deacons that lead straight to the heart of the Christian mission. Many examples come to mind, such as their concern for foreigners and those without a homeland, for the lonely and the poor, for the elderly and the sick, as well as their collaboration in the nursing home movement. Finally, there are also many other needs that are not spoken of quite as often, from drug consumption and alcohol addiction to a lack of direction, lack of motivation, and desperation. Even when deacons take on other duties, such as those expressed by the Council, the main and privileged heart of his task must always be there. This is also a fundamental concern of every bishop. Karl Rahner wrote: "In my opinion, it is the express duty of the bishop to make Christ's love present in the world for all those who suffer, the poor and the weak, the persecuted, etc. Now, in this task of utmost importance, the deacon participates no less than any other priest."

The deacon is in a position of mediation with reality that allows the bishop to focus his efforts on his primary tasks of evangelization and prayer, and that allows men in the Church to bring the history of mankind to the altar of God for the full offering, especially that history in which the contrast, contradiction, and dullness of the world are best expressed, namely the history of the poor. We all know that the development and purification of the Church's self-awareness, especially in our time, has been accompanied by the centrality of service to the poor, and that this service is the Church's primary task in the transition that she must make from self-awareness to the practice of the Christian life. We also know that the terms for what has been defined the "preferential option for the poor" have been clarified, in that this option means to be on the side of the poor by standing with the poor.

The communication of the Gospel must be lived in a world that is characterized by change. We must be aware of this change, we must study it. More importantly, we must implement and develop the sensibility required to develop this awareness. We must also develop our knowledge of the dynamisms that could subtly bring us to think of the ministry of the diaconate as an escape niche, a consideration that is certainly erroneous and pernicious. After all, in the Church and in the world, the deacon, like anybody, is the one who serves.

The deacon moves with greater ease in the contradiction of the world. Thus, he is the one who can remind those who are with him in the Sacred Order to accept this contradiction with the Passion of Jesus, Crucified and Risen. The effort that the deacon makes to overcome the virulence of this contradiction first in himself makes him a luminous and convincing example of the dispossession that is needed for those who wish to put themselves at the service of the Gospel and the poor.

The sacramental grace received in Ordination is the condition of the ordained minister and, at the same time, of the man who lives the so-called "secular" experiences where his family, profession, work, and commitment to society make the deacon particularly suitable for making visible the mystery of the Incarnation, especially on the frontiers, where the future of man and society is determined, and along the paths that the New Evangelization is currently called to take.

This is why it is easier for the deacon to "leave the temple" and become a man on the road from Jerusalem to Jericho, or from Jerusalem to Emmaus, to become a Good Samaritan and a travel companion of those who are tormented by doubt and fear and the many questions surrounding the truth of God and man and the meaning of the present and the future.

We must really emphasize the importance of this aspect so that the deacon does not close himself off in the sacred, so he does not retreat into intimate-devotional forms or exhaust his service in limited groups of people similar to him or members of the association or movement where his vocation may come from, or in small circles of so-called churchgoers. Rather, he must become a minister of the Church that is called—as John Paul II liked to say—to find herself "outside" herself.

We are deacons, and the awareness that *we are in the world, but not of the world* certainly does not exempt us from making concrete effort toward justice and peace. Our journey to encounter brothers, our bending down like Christ over the sufferings and the cry of the poor, our listening, assistance, sharing, and even our bringing the poverties of the world to the altar of Christ cannot deter us from seeking the true and deep causes of discrimination and injustice. And so, our ministry can even give new meaning to the activities of "earthly cities" by constantly reminding politics of its dimension of service to remove causes of injustice and to seek the common good. Also, if I may add, is there a charity, by any chance, that we could more properly define as "politics," which is subject every day to the torment of difficult choices, the struggle of misunderstandings, and the trouble of being a "sign of contradiction" in the world? It is well known that the political sphere is, unfortunately, the one that is most exposed to the dehumanizing temptations of power and possession.

"The Church cannot and must not take upon herself the political battle to bring about the most just society possible. She cannot and must not replace the State. Yet at the same time she cannot and must not remain on the sidelines in the fight for justice. She has to play her part through rational argument and she has to reawaken the spiritual energy without which justice, which always demands sacrifice, cannot prevail and prosper. A just society must be the achievement of politics, not of the Church. Yet the promotion of justice through efforts to bring about openness of mind and will to the demands of the common good is something which concerns the Church deeply."[191]

This is precisely why we must reiterate the *diaconal function* of public engagement, a function that must highlight service to man in accordance with some fundamental values, the main ones being

- *Respect for human dignity*: the first service that is expected of political charity is the respect for human rights and for the minimum conditions for life in community.
- *Creation of concrete conditions that allow everyone to have active participation in the life of society*: wherever there are marginalized people or groups that have *neither voice nor choice*, charity is violated.
- *Service in favor of the disadvantaged*: greater participation of the marginalized and those in

---

191 Pope Benedict XVI, *Deus Caritas Est*, no. 28a.

situations of hardship in the political and economic processes should be the constant objective of political engagement understood as service in favor of the weakest.

- *Commitment to a more equitable distribution of resources and the opportunity to work for all people*: fighting against injustice and inequality in the distribution of goods is the duty of all citizens, but it becomes more effective when it passes through government action and political engagement.

This requires Churches to pay greater attention to the ministry of deacons and to care for and support formation in definite, structurally clear, and permanent terms so they may respond to the needs of men.

In Benedict XVI's Encyclical *Spe Salvi*, he invites us to reflect on Christian *hope*. To be heralds of this hope, deacons must make the experience of the deacon *Philip* their own. The words of the Lord spoken by the angel—*Be ready to set out along the road*—are especially relevant for deacons. Indeed, obeying the order to set out along the road must become a natural answer for deacons, who combine the clerical character of the sacrament with the lay character of the condition of life and who, in a way, are already on the road. We must run up ahead to meet people where they are and, while walking beside them, give them the opportunity to invite us to climb on board. The scene where Philip gets into the Ethiopian's chariot, listens to his questions, and gives him answers is very significant. So, we must live the diaconia of hope intensely where we are, but we must *be ready to set out along the road* even when the road seems deserted; we must *run up ahead* to meet people where they are, walk beside them, listen to them, and talk to them. There is also an inseparable and vital relationship between the *diaconal ministry* and *peace*. Thus, we can rightly say that the way of the diaconate today finds its *needle's eye* in the diaconia of peace and of the poor. As the first to be disarmed, deacons are called to make their Churches "disarmed" as well, *disarmed in penance, in conversation, and in shared charity, recognizing the way of peace that is the way of the Cross and of love.*

Deacons fulfill this specific mission when they join in their lives liturgical service and charitable activity, the *Eucharist* and the *diaconia of the poor*, bearing witness before all that Christ's charity needs the "apron of service." The poor, together with the Eucharist, are the living flesh of Christ.

# The Words of Pope Francis

## Let Us Love, Not with Words But with Deeds

1. "Little children, let us not love in word or speech, but in deed and in truth" (1 Jn 3:18). These words of the Apostle John voice an imperative that no Christian may disregard. The seriousness with which the "beloved disciple" hands down Jesus' command to our own day is made even clearer by the contrast between the empty words so frequently on our lips and the concrete deeds against which we are called to measure ourselves. Love has no alibi. Whenever we set out to love as Jesus loved, we have to take the Lord as our example; especially when it comes to loving the poor. The Son of God's way of loving is well-known, and John spells it out clearly. It stands on two pillars: God loved us first (cf. 1 Jn 4:10, 19), and he loved us by giving completely of himself, even to laying down his life (cf. 1 Jn 3:16).

Such love cannot go unanswered. Even though offered unconditionally, asking nothing in return, it so sets hearts on fire that all who experience it are led to love back, despite their limitations and sins. Yet this can only happen if we welcome God's grace, his merciful charity, as fully as possible into our hearts, so that our will and even our emotions are drawn to love both God and neighbor.

In this way, the mercy that wells up—as it were—from the heart of the Trinity can shape our lives and bring forth compassion and works of mercy for the benefit of our brothers and sisters in need.

2. "This poor man cried, and the Lord heard him" (Ps 34:6). The Church has always understood the importance of this cry. We possess an outstanding testimony to this in the very first pages of the Acts of the Apostles, where Peter asks that seven men, "full of the Spirit and of wisdom" (6:3), be chosen for the ministry of caring for the poor.

This is certainly one of the first signs of the entrance of the Christian community upon the world's stage: the service of the poor. The earliest community realized that being a disciple of Jesus meant demonstrating fraternity and solidarity, in obedience to the Master's proclamation that the poor are blessed and heirs to the Kingdom of heaven (cf. Mt 5:3).

"They sold their possessions and goods and distributed them to all, as any had need" (Acts 2:45). In these words, we see clearly expressed the lively concern of the first Christians. The evangelist Luke, who more than any other speaks of mercy, does not exaggerate when he describes the practice of sharing in the early community. On the contrary, his words are addressed to believers in every generation, and thus also to us, in order to sustain our own witness and to encourage our care for those most in need.

The same message is conveyed with similar conviction by the Apostle James. In his Letter, he spares no words: "Listen, my beloved brethren. Has not God chosen those who are poor in the world to be rich in faith and heirs of the kingdom that he has promised to those who love him? But you have dishonored the poor man. Is it not the rich who oppress you, and drag you into court? . . . What does it profit, my brethren, if a man says he has faith but has not works? Can his faith save him? If a brother or sister is poorly clothed and in lack of daily food, and one of you says to them, 'Go in peace, be warmed and filled,' without giving them the things needed for the body; what does it profit? So faith by itself, if it has not works, is dead" (2:5-6, 14-17).

3. Yet there have been times when Christians have not fully heeded this appeal, and have assumed a worldly way of thinking. Yet the Holy Spirit has not failed to call them to keep their gaze fixed on what is essential. He has raised up men and women who, in a variety of ways, have devoted their lives to the service of the poor. Over these two thousand years, how many pages of history have been written by Christians who, in utter simplicity and humility, and with generous and creative charity, have served their poorest brothers and sisters!

The most outstanding example is that of Francis of Assisi, followed by many other holy men and women over the centuries. He was not satisfied to embrace lepers and give them alms, but chose to go to Gubbio to stay with them. He saw this meeting as the turning point of his conversion: "When I was in my sins, it seemed a thing too bitter to look on lepers, and the Lord himself led me among them and I showed them mercy. And when I left them, what had seemed bitter to me was changed into sweetness of mind and body" (Text 1-3: FF 110). This testimony shows the transformative power of charity and the Christian way of life.

We may think of the poor simply as the beneficiaries of our occasional volunteer work, or of impromptu acts of generosity that appease our conscience. However good and useful such acts may be for making us sensitive to people's needs and the injustices that are often their cause, they ought to lead to a true encounter with the poor and a sharing that becomes a way of life. Our prayer and our journey of discipleship and conversion find the confirmation of their evangelic authenticity in precisely such charity and sharing. This way of life gives rise to joy and peace of soul, because we touch with our own hands the flesh of Christ. If we truly wish to encounter Christ, we have to touch his body in the suffering bodies of the poor, as a response to the sacramental communion bestowed in the Eucharist. The Body of Christ, broken in the sacred liturgy, can be seen, through charity and sharing, in the faces and persons of the most vulnerable of our brothers and sisters. St. John Chrysostom's admonition remains ever timely: "If you want to honor the body of Christ, do not scorn it when it is naked; do not honor the Eucharistic Christ with silk vestments, and then, leaving the church, neglect the other Christ suffering from cold and nakedness" (*Hom. in Matthaeum*, 50.3: PG 58).

We are called, then, to draw near to the poor, to encounter them, to meet their gaze, to embrace them and to let them feel the warmth of love that breaks through their solitude. Their outstretched hand is also an invitation to step out of our certainties and comforts, and to acknowledge the value of poverty in itself.

4. Let us never forget that, for Christ's disciples, poverty is above all a call to follow Jesus in his own poverty. It means walking behind him and beside him, a journey that leads to the beatitude of the Kingdom of heaven (cf. Mt 5:3; Lk 6:20). Poverty means having a humble heart that accepts our creaturely limitations and sinfulness and thus enables us to overcome the temptation to feel omnipotent and immortal. Poverty is an interior attitude that avoids looking upon money, career and luxury as our goal in life and the condition for our happiness. Poverty instead creates the conditions for freely shouldering our personal and social responsibilities, despite our limitations, with trust in God's closeness and the support of his grace. Poverty, understood in this way, is the yardstick that allows us to judge how best to use material goods and to build relationships that

are neither selfish nor possessive (cf. *Catechism of the Catholic Church*, nos. 25-45).

Let us, then, take as our example St. Francis and his witness of authentic poverty. Precisely because he kept his gaze fixed on Christ, Francis was able to see and serve him in the poor. If we want to help change history and promote real development, we need to hear the cry of the poor and commit ourselves to ending their marginalization. At the same time, I ask the poor in our cities and our communities not to lose the sense of evangelical poverty that is part of their daily life.

5. We know how hard it is for our contemporary world to see poverty clearly for what it is. Yet in myriad ways poverty challenges us daily, in faces marked by suffering, marginalization, oppression, violence, torture and imprisonment, war, deprivation of freedom and dignity, ignorance and illiteracy, medical emergencies and shortage of work, trafficking and slavery, exile, extreme poverty and forced migration. Poverty has the face of women, men and children exploited by base interests, crushed by the machinations of power and money. What a bitter and endless list we would have to compile were we to add the poverty born of social injustice, moral degeneration, the greed of a chosen few, and generalized indifference!

Tragically, in our own time, even as ostentatious wealth accumulates in the hands of the privileged few, often in connection with illegal activities and the appalling exploitation of human dignity, there is a scandalous growth of poverty in broad sectors of society throughout our world. Faced with this scenario, we cannot remain passive, much less resigned. There is a poverty that stifles the spirit of initiative of so many young people by keeping them from finding work. There is a poverty that dulls the sense of personal responsibility and leaves others to do the work while we go looking for favors. There is a poverty that poisons the wells of participation and allows little room for professionalism; in this way it demeans the merit of those who do work and are productive. To all these forms of poverty we must respond with a new vision of life and society.

All the poor—as Blessed Paul VI loved to say—belong to the Church by "evangelical right" (Address at the Opening of the Second Session of the Second Vatican Ecumenical Council, September 29, 1963), and require of us a fundamental option on their behalf. Blessed, therefore, are the open hands that embrace the poor and help them: they are hands that bring hope. Blessed are the hands that reach beyond every barrier of culture, religion and nationality, and pour the balm of consolation over the wounds of humanity.

Blessed are the open hands that ask nothing in exchange, with no "ifs" or "buts" or "maybes": they are hands that call down God's blessing upon their brothers and sisters.

6. At the conclusion of the Jubilee of Mercy, I wanted to offer the Church a World Day of the Poor, so that throughout the world Christian communities can become an ever greater sign of Christ's charity for the least and those most in need. To the World Days instituted by my Predecessors, which are already a tradition in the life of our communities, I wish to add this one, which adds to them an exquisitely evangelical fullness, that is, Jesus' preferential love for the poor.

I invite the whole Church, and men and women of good will everywhere, to turn their gaze on this day to all those who stretch out their hands and plead for our help and solidarity. They are our brothers and sisters, created and loved by the one Heavenly Father. This Day is meant, above all, to encourage believers to react against a culture of discard and waste, and to embrace the culture of encounter. At the same time, everyone, independent of religious affiliation, is invited to openness and sharing with the poor through concrete signs of solidarity and fraternity. God created the heavens and the earth for all; yet sadly some have erected barriers, walls and fences, betraying the original gift meant for all humanity, with none excluded.

7. It is my wish that, in the week preceding the World Day of the Poor, which falls this year on November 19, the Thirty-third Sunday of Ordinary Time, Christian communities will make every effort to create moments of encounter and friendship, solidarity and concrete

assistance. They can invite the poor and volunteers to take part together in the Eucharist on this Sunday, in such a way that there be an even more authentic celebration of the Solemnity of Our Lord Jesus Christ, Universal King, on the following Sunday. The kingship of Christ is most evident on Golgotha, when the Innocent One, nailed to the cross, poor, naked and stripped of everything, incarnates and reveals the fullness of God's love. Jesus' complete abandonment to the Father expresses his utter poverty and reveals the power of the Love that awakens him to new life on the day of the Resurrection.

This Sunday, if there are poor people where we live who seek protection and assistance, let us draw close to them: it will be a favorable moment to encounter the God we seek. Following the teaching of Scripture (cf. Gn 18:3-5; Heb 13:2), let us welcome them as honored guests at our table; they can be teachers who help us live the faith more consistently. With their trust and readiness to receive help, they show us in a quiet and often joyful way, how essential it is to live simply and to abandon ourselves to God's providence.

8. At the heart of all the many concrete initiatives carried out on this day should always be prayer. Let us not forget that the Our Father is the prayer of the poor. Our asking for bread expresses our entrustment to God for our basic needs in life. Everything that Jesus taught us in this prayer expresses and brings together the cry of

all who suffer from life's uncertainties and the lack of what they need. When the disciples asked Jesus to teach them to pray, he answered in the words with which the poor speak to our one Father, in whom all acknowledge themselves as brothers and sisters. The Our Father is a prayer said in the plural: the bread for which we ask is "ours," and that entails sharing, participation and joint responsibility. In this prayer, all of us recognize our need to overcome every form of selfishness, in order to enter into the joy of mutual acceptance.

9. I ask my brother Bishops, and all priests and deacons who by their vocation have the mission of supporting the poor, together with all consecrated persons and all associations, movements and volunteers everywhere, to help make this World Day of the Poor a tradition that concretely contributes to evangelization in today's world.

This new World Day, therefore, should become a powerful appeal to our consciences as believers, allowing us to grow in the conviction that sharing with the poor enables us to understand the deepest truth of the Gospel. The poor are not a problem: they are a resource from which to draw as we strive to accept and practice in our lives the essence of the Gospel.

Message for the First World Day of the Poor
Tuesday, June 13, 2017

# Conclusion

The message that Pope Francis gives us on the diaconal ministry speaks of the diaconate's bond with life. Now that we have gone over the pope's words, it is time to provide the ministry of the diaconate with the references it needs to live in the Church and world today. So here are a few final thoughts, though the list is not exhaustive.

In Chapter 6 of the Acts of the Apostles, the figure of the deacon originates from a need in the Church and among the faithful. "The vocation of the deacon is a call to service"—affirms Pope Francis—"service for Jesus Christ, service for the Church, and service to brothers, especially the poorest and those most in need."

As for every other reality of the Church, identity is defined according to the double principle of fidelity to God and fidelity to man. The divine institutions are always, according to the dynamisms of the Incarnation and of salvation, for us and for our salvation. So, we must turn our attention toward the salvation of man, *hic et nunc*, because it is man, in the unrepeatable concreteness of his history, who is at the center of attention in God's heart.

The effect of the council is that, in the *totally ministerial* Church, the "ecclesiastical ministry" that is transmitted with the Sacrament of Holy Orders is in continuity with the everyday pastoral solicitude of the Apostles and is its natural and effective prolongation in the history of mankind and of the People of God. In Buenos Aires, Cardinal Bergoglio focuses on "the requests of the people," that is, what the people ask of ordained ministers. Mostly that they are "docile to the motions of the Spirit, that they are nourished by the Word of God, the Eucharist, and prayer" and "that they are missionaries moved by pastoral charity" in communion with their bishops in order to be "servants of life, alert to the needs of the poorest, committed to the defense of the rights of the weakest, and promoters of the culture of solidarity."[192]

Pope Francis's plan is one of diaconal ministerial life, and in his speeches, he communicates not only his previous pastoral experience, but more importantly, his call to seize this moment of grace that the Church is living to begin a new stage of the journey of evangelization with faith, conviction, and enthusiasm.

The **first step**: First of all, it is necessary to bring the ecclesial mediation of *diaconia* to light more often and in a better way. Unless we wish to destroy the very nature of the Church, this dimension cannot be eliminated. The Second Vatican Council made it clear to everyone that the Church does not identify itself with the Kingdom, but that it is a people convoked in view of the Kingdom. The Church is the way to the Kingdom, a sign of the Kingdom. When the mystery of the Spirit that acts in

---

192 *Aparecida* Document, no. 199.

the world protects and envelops the People of God, it transcends and overcomes it in the salvation of humanity. Above all else, this Church is *kerygma*, the Word of God in the world. It is prophecy. It is the evangelization of the generations throughout the centuries. This proclamation, however, finds its experiential tangibility in the life of the Church, which is also *koinonia*, fraternal community, that is, unity in communication and communion, a blessed place where "peace" and "love" are not empty words, but rather the anticipation and first fruits of the Kingdom. *Kerygma* and new life are obviously celebrated by the People of God. For this reason, the Church is also liturgy: feasts, sacraments, prayer. But this is not enough. "This means"—in the words of the pope—"that there must always be a profound awareness that one is not bishop, priest or deacon because he is more intelligent, worthier or better than other men; he is such only pursuant to a gift, a gift of love bestowed by God, through the power of his Spirit, for the good of his people."[193] The People of God, who have been inserted into a world that is called to communion with God, but who are currently extraneous to his project of love, have an essential and unavoidable relationship with the society in which they live: they are leaven for the dough and a positive relationship of sympathy, not condemnation and anathema. The Church is an attitude of *diaconia*,

---

193 Pope Francis, General Audience (November 12, 2014).

of service to man, in the wake of her Lord who came *to serve and not to be served.* Thus, the People of God become service, human promotion, gestures of the Good Samaritan, liberation from oppression, education, and the fight for justice. With the Council, all of this seemed to be received patrimony, almost common consciousness. However, the dangers inherent in *diaconia,* the implications—even political—that it entails, and the "dirtying of the hands" involved in coming into contact with history create so much uncertainty that it seems much more peaceable to take refuge in the *kerygma* and Liturgy, or perhaps to live unity in small groups or reduce *diaconia* to simple acts of assistance, as in past centuries. It is quite evident that if this temptation became his life, the deacon would not have very much to do. He could wear the white tunic, but that's about as far as it would go. His contact with the world would be useless. His being a "Church at the service" in the society of men would be mute and meaningless.

Times like ours—this is the **second step**—require more room to be made for a *Church that is evangelically open to the world.* "And today we see"—Francis says— "that in addition to the twelve Apostles he calls another seventy-two, and sends them to the villages, two by two, to proclaim that the Kingdom of God is close at hand. This is very beautiful! Jesus does not want to act alone, he came to bring the love of God into the world and he wants to spread it in the style of communion, in the style of brotherhood. That is why he immediately forms a community of disciples, which is a missionary community. He trains them straight away for the mission, to go forth. . . . How many missionaries do this, they sow life, health, comfort to the outskirts of the world."[194]

The diaconate was born in the optimistic climate of a Church that distanced herself from "prophets of doom" and that saw signs of God's salvific love in creation and in history. This Church speaks to men of good will; she addresses their deepest thoughts where reasoning, honesty, and the desire for fullness make each man an ally of God, whether he knows it or not. These are the men that the Church wants to serve; it is with them that she wants to build the Kingdom, no matter what culture they belong to.

The **third step** for a future face of the deacon is to try is found in the need that the Church has in the modern world to *declericalize*. Francis says: "There is the danger of clericalism: the deacon who is too clerical. No, no, this is not good. At times I see someone who assists at the liturgy: it almost seems as if he wants to take the place of the priest. Clericalism, beware of clericalism. And another temptation is functionalism: it is a help that the priest has for this or that; a boy to carry out certain tasks and not for other things. No. You have a clear charism in the Church and you must build it.

---

194 Pope Francis, *Angelus* (July 7, 2013).

The diaconate is a specific vocation, a family vocation that requires service."[195] It is not a matter of becoming increasingly more aware of the decrease in and the structural crisis of those called to the priesthood; it is a matter of making a Church that has all too often over the centuries transferred every function and every charism to priests and bishops become more a "People of God."

Pope Francis's invitation to declericalization urges deacons to put themselves at the "service to God and to brothers. And how far we have to go in this sense! You are the guardians of service in the Church. Therein lies the value of the charisms in the Church, which are a memory and a gift for helping all the people of God not to lose the perspective and wealth of God's action. You are not half priests, half laypeople—this would be to 'functionalize' the diaconate—you are the sacrament of service to God and to others. And from this word 'service' there derives all the development of your work, of your vocation, of your being within the Church."

The **fourth step** for looking for the face of the deacon of the future is the rediscovery in the Church of an option that is becoming ever more urgent and inescapable. We are referring to the conciliar concept of the Church as a community that commits to the "option for the poor." "Our deacon, the deacon of this diocese, Deacon Lawrence—the 'treasurer of the diocese'—who,

195  Pope Francis, Pastoral Visit (March 25, 2017).

when the emperor asked him to bring the riches of the diocese to turn them over in order to avoid being killed, St. Lawrence returned with the poor. The poor are the treasure of the Church."[196]

We have come so far since the famous conciliar affirmations (LG, no. 8) and Paul VI's lapidary expression, "the poor are a sacrament of Christ"! In the opulent West, defining ourselves as a Church of the poor that chooses the poor as her sacrament meant setting many Christians up for martyrdom. It also meant distancing ourselves from a history that is too abundantly marked by the demands of profit and the market as well as becoming an antagonist to those who still base their hegemony and well-being on exploitation and injustice. This progress now continues through the work of Francis, who speaks to us and puts concrete signs into practice because, as he writes in *Evangelii Gaudium*, he wants a poor Church for the poor and, so, a Church that is truly *diaconal*. The pope even says that "there is no altar service, there is no liturgy that is not open to the poor, and there no service to the poor that does not lead to the liturgy."[197]

Realistically, there has yet to be a change of course in the mentality of many deacons who are tenacious defenders of their own rights and of cultivating their

---

196 Pope Francis, Homily (December 15, 2015).

197 Pope Francis, Pastoral Visit (March 25, 2017).

own gardens. It is the way that we look at things, that is, our mentality, our diaconia, or the way we embody our diaconia, if you will. We must instead be rooted in the Gospel of Jesus: "Love"—Francis writes—"has no alibi. Whenever we set out to love as Jesus loved, we have to take the Lord as our example; especially when it comes to loving the poor."[198] For this reason, the pope invites deacons to make themselves "available in life, meek of heart and in constant dialogue with Jesus[;] you will not be afraid to be *servants of Christ*, and to encounter and caress the flesh of the Lord in the poor of our time."[199] The icon that we are presented with is the deacon Stephen; "the book of the Acts of the Apostles presents him to us as 'a man full of faith and of the Holy Spirit' (6:5), chosen with six others for the service of widows and the poor in the first Community of Jerusalem."[200]

The **fifth** and final **step** summarizes the previous steps and perceives a renewed commitment to evangelization in the thought of Pope Francis, who affirms that "missionary outreach is paradigmatic for all the Church's activity."[201] This is why it is necessary to seize this favorable moment in order to catch sight of and live out this

---

198  Pope Francis, First World Day of the Poor, no. 1.

199  Pope Francis, Homily (May 29, 2016).

200  Pope Francis, *Angelus* (December 26, 2013).

201  EG, no. 15.

"new stage" of evangelization. Therefore, we must look to the future, despite this moment of crisis, so we can once again make a "banner of victory" out of the Cross and Resurrection of Christ.

So, we have to stop complaining only about the growing inhumanity spreading throughout the world and the violence that is becoming a more and more "ordinary" way of life. We must accept the challenge that is the immense task of *evangelization*, or, as Francis says, "experience"—as deacons—"the evangelization of the peripheries."[202] Cardinal Bergoglio told the pastoral council in his diocese that "mission becomes the paradigm of all evangelizing action."[203] The Latin American experience led the archbishop of Buenos Aires to say that "despite the irreligiousness that reigns in parishes, the response coming from suburban chapels and basic communities served by deacons, religious men and women, and the laity continue to be a space for communion, participation, and socialization, authentic evangelization, catechesis, and the practice of lay

202 Pope Francis, Message for the Fifty-Third World Day of Prayer for Vocations.

203 Words of Cardinal Jorge Mario Bergoglio, Archbishop of Buenos Aires, First Meeting with the Presbyteral Council 2008, April 15, 2008, *Agencia Informativa Católica Argentina* (AICA), in Spanish: *http://aica.org/aica/documentos_files/Obispos_Argentinos/Bergoglio/2008/2008_04_15.html* (accessed May 4, 2018).

ministries."[204] If we do not open our eyes to the radical conversion that is asking the Church to carry out her task of Gospel proclamation, and so, her mission of education, then even evangelization is useless and sterile. "Personal conversion"—observes Bergoglio, along with the bishops of Latin America—"engenders the ability to make everything subject to establishing the Kingdom of life. . . . Bishops, priests, permanent deacons, religious men and women, and lay men and women are all called to assume an attitude of ongoing pastoral conversion, which entails listening attentively and discerning 'what the Spirit says to the churches' (Rev 2:29) through the signs of the times in which God is made manifest."[205] "Conversion and vocation are two sides of the same coin, and continually remain interconnected throughout the whole of the missionary disciple's life."[206]

We should not think of a deacon's family as the family of a "half-priest." The pope cautions us repeatedly, saying that we must "be careful not to see deacons as half priests, half laypeople. This is a danger. At the end they will end up neither one nor the other. No, we must not do this, it is a danger. Looking at them in this way

204 Card. Jorge Mario Bergoglio, SJ, Presentation by the Archbishop at the V Conference of CELAM, Aparecida, May 2007, *Arzobispado de Buenos Aires*, in Spanish: *http://www.arzbaires.org.ar/inicio/homilias/homilias2007.htm* (accessed May 4, 2018).

205 Aparecida Concluding Document, no. 366. *http://www.celam.org/aparecida/Ingles.pdf* (accessed amy 4, 2018).

206 Message for the Fifty-Third World Day of Prayer for Vocations.

harms us and harms them. This way of considering them takes strength from the charism proper to the diaconate."[207] Instead, we should think of the deacon's family as a workshop where he is helped to be "other" than the world around us, to be different, that is, "holy." It is a workshop where enthusiasm for one's baptismal identity is not a reason for confrontation or exclusion, but the awareness of having something to say to the world: a "word" that echoes the "Word" and that becomes richness that welcomes and that is given to others.

"Holy Orders, in its three grades of bishop, priest and deacon, is the Sacrament that enables a man to exercise the ministry which the Lord Jesus entrusted to the Apostles, to shepherd his flock, in the power of his Spirit and according to his Heart."[208]

The in-depth analysis of the sacramentality of the diaconate has certainly been one of the most interesting elements of theological reflection on the diaconate in these post-conciliar years. The International Theological Commission's document *From the Diakonia of Christ to the Diakonia of the Apostles* devotes all of Chapter IV and part of Chapter VII to this topic. Part II of Chapter VII discusses the "Implications of the Sacramentality of the Diaconate," and there is an attitude of immediate

---

207 Pope Francis, Pastoral Visit (March 23, 2017).

208 Pope Francis, General Audience (March 26, 2014).

openness and careful reflection regarding this matter that should be carefully reconsidered.

Therefore, "In the presence and in the ministry of the bishops, of the priests and deacons"—the pope writes—"we can recognize the true face of the Church: it is the Hierarchical Holy Mother Church. And truly, through these brothers chosen by the Lord and consecrated through the Sacrament of Holy Orders, the Church exercises her motherhood: she gives birth to us in Baptism as Christians, giving us a new birth in Christ; she watches over our growth in the faith; she accompanies us into the arms of the Father, to receive his forgiveness; she prepares the Eucharistic table for us, where she nourishes us with the Word of God and the Body and Blood of Jesus; she invokes upon us the blessing of God and the power of his Spirit, sustaining us throughout the course of our life and enveloping us with her tenderness and warmth, especially in those most delicate moments of trial, of suffering and of death."[209]

In concluding this work, a special thanks goes to Pope Francis who, in his homily for the Jubilee of Deacons, thanked deacons for their presence in the Church, and at the same time, entrusted the life and ministry of all deacons throughout the world to the Virgin Mary. He entrusts deacons, on the other hand, with a new diaconal service: we must not forget to pray for he who has

---

209 Pope Francis, General Audience (November 5, 2014).

told us since the beginning of his papacy that he wants a poor Church for the poor, and therefore, a Church that is diaconal.

# Afterword

This book offers readers for the first time an extensive collection of Pope Francis's writings on the diaconate. It includes letters, homilies, speeches, and messages addressed to the faithful, to priests, and to deacons during celebrations, Angeluses, national and international conventions, and audiences from Jorge Mario Bergoglio's time as archbishop of Buenos Aires and now as pope. These works have been grouped into thirteen sections; in the first three, the author focuses on the diaconate in the Papal Magisterium and in the thought of Pope Francis, while the remaining parts are dedicated to the writings of Cardinal Bergoglio and the pope, respectively.

In these texts, we find the heart of Pope Francis's overall vision on the diaconal ministry, which influenced his service during his time as archbishop and which continues to influence his thought and actions today as pope. These texts reflect on how the diaconate interfaces with the ecclesiology of communion, the result of conciliar Magisterium, and on how the diaconate produces its best results in pastoral work, which is built on personal and networked relationships, topics that Cardinal Bergoglio had already expounded upon in his magisterium as archbishop.

As pope, Francis reminds deacons to be "custodians of service" and "meek and humble servants of Christ and brothers" in the Church. At an audience on Wednesday, November 12, 2014, he cautioned the "hierarchy," saying "there would be problems if a bishop, a priest or a deacon thought he knew everything, that he always had the right answer for everything and did not need anyone. On the contrary, awareness that he, as the first recipient of the mercy and compassion of God, should lead a minister of the Church to always be humble and sympathetic with respect to others. Also, in the awareness of being called to bravely guard the faith entrusted (cf. 1 Tm 6:20), he shall listen to the people."

It is the special attention given to the current situation of the poor and immigrants, prefiguring the model of a Church that is poor and close to the poorest, that has characterized his papacy from the beginning.

In reference to the diaconate, we like to repeat a solicitude of Pope Francis that invites us to assume a mindset marked by "restlessness, incompleteness, imagination." This recommendation presents the diaconal ministry with a challenge from the pope and solicits courageous theological research that is the product of an open and flexible mind that is not limited to re-proposing a ministry from the past, but one that is capable of service that keeps up with the times and that is able to read the changing "signs of the times" throughout history and the ecclesial journey.

The author's research is a *truly diaconal* investigation that involves all the components of the Church: the People of God, theologians, and pastors.

The aim of this book is to evaluate the fundamental principles at the basis of the diaconate in light of the thought of Pope Francis in order to determine not only whether the restoration of the permanent diaconate has proven to be useful, but more importantly, what characteristics the diaconate must have to respond to the demands of today's global and social situations.

Pope Francis had this to say in Milan on March 25: "You are not half priests, half laypeople—this would be to 'functionalize' the diaconate—you are the sacrament of service to God and to others. And from this word 'service' there derives all the development of your work, of your vocation, of your being within the Church. A vocation that, like all vocations is not only individual, but lived within the family and with the family; within the People of God and with the People of God."[210]

Therefore, we must do away with the erroneous, yet very common idea that the restoration of the diaconate was a response to a scarcity of clergy and that deacons are like half-priests or failed priests. On the contrary, the diaconate has its own specific role; it is part of the Church structure. So, even in a situation where there

---

210 Pope Francis, Pastoral Visit (March 23, 2017).

are enough priests, the absence of deacons always leaves a void.

The deacon is the one who, by the sacramental grace consistent with the character of his Ordination, is meant to be a servant of the Christian people and of humanity, in imitation of Christ.

Undoubtedly, all Christians are called to service, but the function of the deacon is to be consecrated to service by virtue of his Ordination and so, to be a tangible sign of Christ the deacon (a servant), endowed with a mission of witness, the mission of arousing the diaconal spirit (the spirit of service) throughout the Church. So, just as there is a ministerial priesthood proper to priests together with the common priesthood of the faithful, there is also a ministerial service proper to deacons with the common service to which all the faithful are called. The areas where the deacon's service is exercised are those assigned to him by ecclesiastical tradition, but the pope says that the deacon is "at the service for Jesus Christ, service for the Church, and service to brothers, especially the poorest and those most in need. Don't be "part-time deacons" or functionaries. The Church is not an NGO. May service enhance your lives."[211] This ministry is the deacon's richness because it is a consequence of his openness to service.

---

211 Pope Francis, Letter to Deacons in Buenos Aires on the Day of their Ordination (March 16, 2013).

Another observation that can be made, considering the Magisterium of the pope, is the deficiency in *evangelization*. Echoing throughout this book are words from the Exhortation *Evangelii Gaudium*, which the pope uses to bring about what we can define as a return to the focal point of Christian life. In fact, this "realigning" with the Gospel, from which the burdens of everyday life never cease to distract us, is proper to every renewal of the Church or spiritual return to the source. Indeed, Jesus' words, "Proclaim the gospel to every creature" (Mk 16:15), are to be understood, not only in the sense that the Gospel is to be proclaimed to all peoples, but also in the sense that those who know nothing about Christianity and the Gospel, even those who are baptized Christians, must also be evangelized. Now, unfortunately, it is undeniable that the majority of our population does not know the Gospel, and they live as if God did not exist. The pope writes, "In this Exhortation I wish to encourage the Christian faithful to embark upon a new chapter of evangelization marked by this joy, while pointing out new paths for the Church's journey in years to come."[212] The pope invites bishops, priests, and deacons to "recover the original freshness of the Gospel" while finding "new avenues" and "new paths of creativity."[213] All Christians are called to "go

---

212 EG, no. 1.

213 EG, no. 11.

forth from our own comfort zone in order to reach all the 'peripheries' in need of the light of the Gospel," "all of us are called to take part in this new missionary 'going forth,'"[214] "no one can be excluded."[215] It is about "a pastoral and missionary conversion which cannot leave things as they presently are" and that pushes us to be "permanently in a state of mission."[216]

In the penultimate part, the book considers the reflection on the "diaconia of women" and the recognition of women at all levels of pastoral life in the Church for greater involvement in the participatory and decision-making structures. This book includes words from Pope Francis's audience with the superiors general of congregations of women religious on May 12, 2016, which led to the constitution of a commission to study the female diaconate.

The book closes with the "preferential option for the poor" and the full text from the pope's message on the first World Day of the Poor, which he instituted at the end of the Jubilee of Mercy and which was celebrated on November 19, 2017, with the theme: "Let us love, not with words but with deeds." Pope Francis launches a warning, which the book captures very well, and calls upon deacons in particular to choose "the option for

---

214  EG, no. 20.

215  EG, no. 23.

216  EG, no. 25.

the poor" in their life, because Francis wants a "Church which is poor and for the poor," and so, as the author rightly states, a Church that is "diaconal." So, as the slogan from the Jubilee in May 2016 says, deacons are *dispensers of charity* in the Church and in the world.

This book makes it clear that the diaconate must be seen as the gift of "sacramental grace" destined to "deepen ecclesial communion," to "revive the commitment to mission," to promote "the sense of community and of family spirit of the people of God," and to "accentuate the community and missionary dimensions of the Church and pastoral work" with the aim of "more widespread evangelization for the salvation of humanity."

Edmondo A. Caruana, O. Carm.